Twayne's New Critical Introductions
to Shakespeare

THE WINTER'S
TALE

By the same author

The Dramatist and the Received Idea: Studies in the Plays of Marlowe and Shakespeare (Cambridge University Press, 1968)
John Donne's Poetry (Cambridge University Press, 1971)
Shakespeare's Magnanimity: Four Tragic Heroes, their Friends and Families (with Howard Jacobson) (Chatto & Windus, 1978)

Fiction
Like the Big Wolves (Quartet, 1985)

Twayne's New Critical Introductions to Shakespeare

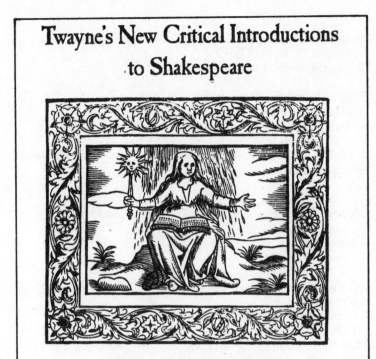

THE WINTER'S TALE

Wilbur Sanders

TWAYNE PUBLISHERS · BOSTON

A Division of G. K. Hall & Co.

Published in the United States by Twayne Publishers,
division of G. K. Hall & Co.,
70 Lincoln Street, Boston, Massachusetts.

Published simultaneously in Great Britain by
The Harvester Press Limited,
16 Ship Street, Brighton, Sussex.

Library of Congress Cataloging-in-Publication Data

Sanders, Wilbur.
    The winter's tale.

    (Twayne's new critical introduction to Shakespeare)
    Bibliography: p.
    1. Shakespeare, William, 1564–1616. Winter's tale.
I. Title.   II. Series.
PR2839.S26   1987   822.3'3   87–21090
ISBN 0–8057–8702–X
ISBN 0–8057–8705–4 (pbk)

Claire Gabrielle Sanders

In memory ... and with love ...

'Bequeath to death your numbness, for from him
Dear life redeems you.'

Titles in the Series

GENERAL EDITOR: GRAHAM BRADSHAW

General Editor's Preface

The *New Critical Introductions to Shakespeare* series will include studies of all Shakespeare's plays, together with two volumes on the non-dramatic verse, and is designed to offer a challenge to all students of Shakespeare.

Each volume will be brief enough to read in an evening, but long enough to avoid those constraints which are inevitable in articles and short essays. Each contributor will develop a sustained critical reading of the play in question, which addresses those difficulties and critical disagreements which each play has generated.

Different plays present different problems, different challenges and excitements. In isolating these, each volume will present a preliminary survey of the play's stage history and critical reception. The volumes then provide a more extended discussion of these matters in the main text, and of matters relating to genre, textual problems and the use of source material, or to historical and theoretical issues. But here, rather than setting a row of dragons at the gate, we have assumed that 'background' should figure only as it emerges into a critical foreground; part of the critical endeavour is to establish, and sift, those issues which seem most pressing.

So, for example, when Shakespeare determined that *his* Othello and Desdemona should have no time to live together, or that Cordelia dies while Hermione survives, his deliberate departures from his source material have a critical significance which is often blurred, when discussed in the context of lengthily detailed surveys of 'the sources'. Alternatively, plays like *The Merchant of Venice* or *Measure for Measure* show Shakespeare welding together different 'stories' from quite different sources, so that their relation to each other becomes a matter for critical debate. And Shakespeare's dramatic practice poses different critical questions when we ask—or if we ask: few do—why particular characters in a poetic drama speak only in verse or only in prose; or when we try to engage with those recent, dauntingly specialised and controversial textual studies which set out to establish the evidence for authorial revisions or joint authorship. We all read *King Lear* and *Macbeth*, but we are not all textual critics; nor are textual critics always able to show where their arguments have critical consequences which concern us all.

Just as we are not all textual critics, we are not all linguists, cultural anthropologists, psychoanalysts or New Historicists. The diversity of contemporary approaches to Shakespeare is unprecedented, enriching, bewildering. One aim of this series is to represent what is illuminating in this diversity. As the hastiest glance through the list of contributors will confirm, the series does not attempt to 're-read' Shakespeare by placing an ideological grid over the text and reporting on whatever shows through. Nor would the series' contributors always agree with each other's arguments, or premises; but each has been invited to develop a sustained critical argument which will also provide its own critical and historical context—by taking account of those issues which have perplexed or divided audiences, readers, and critics past and present.

Graham Bradshaw

Contents

The Stage History

So far as a critical understanding of Shakespeare's art is concerned, the stage history of *The Winter's Tale* is for the most part a history of uncomprehending travesty. Sometimes it makes dismal, sometimes hilarious reading; but I am happy to be able to report that everything pertinent and impertinent, in this connection, has been assembled in Dennis Bartholomeusz's *'The Winter's Tale' in Performance in England and America, 1611–1976*. Anybody whose curiosity is excited to pursue the rash of primpings, prunings and cannibalisations the play has suffered over the centuries will find ample references and documentation in that book.

The most productive spirit in which to approach this tale of misconstruction and misappropriation, it seems to me, is one of lucid inquiry: what is it about Shakespeare's text that has made it so difficult for theatre people to give their audiences what the astute critic maintains is simply *there*? There would seem to be something obstructive in the very grain of the matter, some unresolved difficulty of mode, some opacity in the relation between the 'art' of the play and the 'nature' it inevitably (being a play) represents. Is the play, then, 'a failure'—whatever that would mean? Or is it a 'success' of so unusual a kind, that it taxes the imagination and resourcefulness of our directors in ways they aren't used to encountering? The Stage History, in other words, is most usefully confronted as a concrete manifestation of a knotty critical problem.

The Critical Reception

Some of the most useful remarks concerning *The Winter's Tale* belong to the happy time when the notion of a 'critical reception' had not been dreamt of—palmy, amateur days, these, before the lemon-squeezer became the paradigm of criticism, and when writers who *were* writers set down their reactions without too much caution or premeditation. It is never wasted time to consult these men—Dr Johnson's notes; Coleridge's scattered reflections; Hazlitt's *Characters of Shakespeare's Plays*; nor, I might add, the neglected Dowden (*Shakspere: his Mind and Art*), or Masefield, in his brief but pregnant volume, *William Shakespeare*. The very brevity of these commentaries often gives them a force denied to prolixity.

A sampler of critical opinion from 1611 to 1966 may be found in the *Casebook* edited by Kenneth Muir, where, though the extracts are sometimes maddeningly truncated, it is usually possible to deduce which ones deserve following up. Philip Edwards draws a discriminating map of the twentieth-century critical terrain in his 'Shakespeare's Romances: 1900–1957', printed in *Shakespeare Survey*, 11 (1958); and D.J. Palmer's *Shakespeare's Later Comedies* assembles some other modern essays. All of these publications contain suggestions for further reading, as do most modern editions of the play. I shall not, therefore,

xiv   *The Winter's Tale*

recycle lists which in turn recycle other lists, of which we already have a plentiful supply.

One aspect of the contemporary criticism of *The Winter's Tale*, however, provokes comment: it is an orthodoxy, by turns complacent and ferocious (depending on how threatened it feels), which will have no truck whatsoever with what it calls 'psychologising'. The word is as strange as the distaste it registers: it contrives to suggest that it is somehow naïve or illicit to view drama as a picture of the human psyche in action. Thus Leavis dons his black cap and pronounces savage sentence on any fool-critic who dares to inquire about the cause of Leontes' jealousy. Muir, blandly introducing his selection in the *Casebook*, congratulates himself on totally suppressing 'the error of the psychologising approach'. Others reach the same safe haven sailing by the twin stars of mythos and symbolism: for S.L. Bethell, the play is a straightforward religious allegory in which Perdita is 'symbolically the life of grace that Leontes has lost'; for Glynne Wickham, the allegory is political-historical—'Hermione is Britain, the wife divorced by the first Brutus and mystically restored to the second Brutus (James I)'; and for F.C. Tinckler, Shakespeare has offered us a sophisticated vegetation myth. But whatever the route, the all-important destination has been reached: we now have a sanitised 'Romance' from which all the real people have been hygienically removed. And there will be no more 'psychologising' in future!

Such diktats, of course, have the disadvantage of provoking one, in the spirit of inquiry, to defy them—and rightly so, I think. For it requires no great percipience to see that the hostility to 'psychology' has an idiosyncratic psychology all its own. If our 'psychologising' is inapposite, we can trust the play to tell us so; there's no need for a methodological blockade. Anyway, a Shakespearian text, in my experience, is hospitable to almost any kind of query you care to throw at it, *provided* that you're prepared to rephrase the question continuously in the light of the kind of answer you find you're getting. This I hope to have done.

For Shakespeare's sources, the eighth volume of Geoffrey Bullough's *Narrative and Dramatic Sources of Shakespeare* gives everything one needs, though John Lawlor's article on '*Pandosto* and the Nature of Dramatic Romance' is a helpful supplement, in its careful consideration of the transformation Greene undergoes at Shakespeare's hands.

The Bibliography at the end of this book provides references for all these works, plus a handful of items I'm glad to have read because I found them delightful, or stimulating, or constructively infuriating. My greatest debt, under all three headings, is to Wilson Knight's classic essay in *The Crown of Life*—a piece which is quite wonderfully wrong about most things, and it doesn't matter in the least.

For the text of the play, one can't do better than the unedited Folio. The problem of Jacobean (very possibly Shakespearian) punctuation and syntax, the necessity of *deducing* Stage Directions rather than accepting them passively from editors, the suggestive strangeness of unfamiliar spellings—all these features, preserved in the Folio, are aids to freshness in the reading; and a glance at a modern edition will quickly inform one of the offered solutions to unsolved textual tangles, while keeping open the possibility that they *ought not* to be solved.

Indeed, confronted by critical and theatrical dissension, the Folio text, read in the spirit recommended by its first editors, is the only true court of appeal:

> Reade him, therefore; and againe, and againe: And if then you doe not like him, surely you are in some manifest danger, not to vnderstand him. And so we leaue you to other of his Friends, whom if you need, can bee your guides: if you neede them not, you can leade your selues. And such Readers we wish him.

Still, there is probably no 'manifest danger' in reading the essay that follows. The play will always be there to be read again ... and again.

· 1 ·

The Jealousy of Leontes
Act I

Critics need problems as slugs need cabbages, and I would not blame anyone who tensed in anticipatory resistance when I say that I am writing about *The Winter's Tale* because I find the play problematic. However, I do: I think it wonderful, moving, grand; but I am also niggled by small discontents which have a nasty habit of growing bigger the more I think about them. I don't believe I am alone in this.

For some readers the play is a sublime diptych, a two-movement symphony whose music is only made richer by its overt structural diversity. For others, equally flatly, it is a broken-backed drama, written in two distinct modes, where Shakespeare has stymied himself by trying to do two imcompatible things at once. The dispute, at its most interesting, is about much more important matters than construction, and it's because I take it extremely seriously that I haven't, in what follows, tried to resolve it in any haste. I'm not even sure of the benefits of *having* it resolved; for this is, more than most, a play to be 'wondered at', and wondered over. So if readers find themselves wondering how long the wondering is going to continue, I can only plead a difficulty which I believe to be in the play itself, and hope that I shall have succeeded, by the end, in showing how rich a difficulty it is.

To begin at the beginning, then ... well, almost the

beginning: what is it that happens to Leontes in the second scene of *The Winter's Tale*?

The question has to be asked because readers and audiences, critics and directors keep disagreeing so spectacularly about it. Some of them will even dispute that anything 'happens' to Leontes at all. Inquiring into the matter, they assure us, is as foolish as trying to find out exactly how Cinderella's coach became a pumpkin. Don't we know a fairy tale when we see one? Leontes, patently, has taken a bite of the evil apple which turns a plain good man into a bewitched devil. And for as long as the poison lasts (which is just as long as the fable requires), he will be inaccessible to plain good feelings. The moment the poison is exhausted, he will emerge from his enchantment, bewildered and distraught, scarcely able to recognise the world which is now strewn with the wreckage of his evil possession. End of Phase One: the Triumph of Wickedness. And anyone familiar with the genre will then await, with minimal anxiety, the beginning of Phase Two: the Triumph of Time. That is to say, the deployment of the complementary *good* magic which will, after the usual pleasing delays, undo all the damage and launch us onto the calm, valedictory seas of the happy-ever-after. Easy. There's no problem except the needless one created by treating a tale for the winter fireside as if it were a documentary account of marital conflict in contemporary suburbia. We perplex ourselves with irrelevant speculation about motivation, and thus invent a problem where none exists.

It would be foolish to pretend that Shakespeare's tale doesn't have this shape. It does make some sense to describe the Leontes of I.ii as 'possessed', and he does seem, at the end of the trial scene (III.ii) to awaken, as if from nightmare. In a score of ways the fabular paradigm is visible through the dramatic fabric.

But it is nevertheless a *dramatic* fabric. And in drama things do 'happen'. Where the fairy tale deals in isolated, portentous events, linked only by a narrative 'and then', in drama the event has a location and conditions, causal roots and consequential branches. The actors who encounter each other in that curious acoustic space we call a stage, do so by imitating the forms of encounter that we recognise from other rooms—rooms, even, in contemporary suburbia: they stand nearer to, or further from, each other; they raise or lower their voices; they stress one word rather than another; they reach out to touch each other, or they shrink painfully from contact. And all this we interpret as behaviour—known physical behaviour in which one thing grows out of another. Concerning dramatic events it's the most natural thing in the world to ask (as Polixenes does concerning Leontes' monstrous suspicion, the moment it is revealed to him), 'How should this *grow?*'.

'Natural it may be', comes the retort, 'but with this play the question is illicit. It is only being asked because of a misunderstanding of modes.' This sort of thing:

> There is no psychological interest; we don't ask (so long as we are concerning ourselves with Shakespeare): What elements in Leontes' make-up, working in what way, explain this storm? The question is irrelevant to the mode of the play.
> (F. R. Leavis, *The Common Pursuit*, 1952, p.177)

So that's that. One is sorry one asked. Leavis' argument has all the subtlety of a slammed door. But, pausing for a moment ... how do we establish the 'mode' of a play, if not by reading it first? And why, in a piece which notably shifts modes at its mid-point, should the word 'mode' be in the singular? I don't know who 'we' are, but we seem to make a pretty supine and incurious audience. Before we conclude that Leontes' jealousy is simply a plot postulate, mightn't it be worth inquiring *how* Shakespeare postulates it? It may be 'notoriously unmotivated', as S. L. Bethell claims (*Casebook*, ed. K. Muir, 1968, p.116), only because it has been notoriously unexamined.

I said dramatic events have a location and conditions. And in the first scene—to begin really at the beginning—we are given them. It's an opening that has perplexed directors, and the usual consequence has been that the scene gets cut. Those who don't cut it remain perplexed, it seems; for one ingenious Stratford director was so puzzled by the Sicilian subjects who 'desire to live on crutches', that he actually brought on a bevy of them, complete with crutches, to clear up the difficulty. Perhaps it's worth trying a simpler solution—entertaining the possibility, for instance, that there is a joke in the air, and that the pervasive formality of speech in the scene may not be some Shakespearian lapse upon generic courtliness, but a careful registration of a particular courtly note which helps, in turn, to delineate a particular socio-political situation. What exactly is happening here?

Two courtiers are discussing the progress of Bohemia's visit to Sicilia. And the terms they use suggest a competition in state lavishness rather than an easy munificence born of affection. Archidamus the Bohemian, indeed (who never appears again), seems to be there chiefly to express the embarrassment this ostentatious hospitality is causing his party. He worries how it can ever be requited:

> we cannot with such magnificence, in so rare—I know not what to say. We will give you sleepy drinks, that your senses, unintelligent of our insufficience, may, though they cannot praise us, as little accuse us.
>
> (I.i. 12)

Camillo tries to rescue the entertainment from the suspicion of commercial competition—'You pay a great deal too dear for what's given freely'—but only manages to still his guest's misgivings by appealing to the boyhood friendship, long in the past, which has brought the visit about, and by affirming its continuing and mature solidity. Here perhaps the hospitable contention can come to some rest?

Archidamus, the Bohemian, seems to think so:

I think there is not in the world either malice or matter to alter it.

Perhaps not. And yet when you deny a possibility, you also endow it with equivocal life; and Archidamus is moved, next, to shift his ground, as if to a more 'comfortable' topic:

You have an unspeakable comfort of your young Prince Mamillius.

The 'unspeakable' of courtly hyperbole, however, may yet be spoken of:

it is a gentleman of the greatest promise that ever came into my note.

The greatest *ever?* Well, no doubt he'd say as much for his own young Prince, on the appropriate occasion. But Camillo doesn't quibble. He takes it in the spirit it's offered, abating the hyperbole only a shade in the interests of a modest realism:

I very well agree with you in the *hopes* of him. It is a gallant child.

(On a similar occasion, Hamlet had qualified the praise of his dead father, in order to pay the finer compliment of moderation: 'A was a man, take him for all in all:/ I shall not look upon his like again.')
But hyperbole, once you're entangled in it, is a net of fine meshes, and Camillo is not yet out of it. The royal child is, he assures his guest,

one that indeed physics the subject, makes old hearts fresh; they that went on crutches ere he was born desire yet their life to see him a man.

Archidamus tries briefly to imagine such prodigies of geriatric fealty, fails, and gives it up with a laugh:

Would they else be content to die?

'Yes', replies Camillo stoutly, choosing to impugn his intelligence rather than his loyalty, but avoiding fatuousness by adding a sly proviso:

if there were no other excuse why they should desire to live.

Which allows a sagely nodding Archidamus to administer the *coup de grace*. I see, he says, po-faced,

If the King had *no* son, they would desire to live on crutches till he *had* one.

That kind of loyal subject. Ah yes, we have them in Bohemia too.

Unless it is with an unscripted grin, Camillo doesn't bother to reply. They have returned (with some relief) to the real world. The easy accord, obstructed throughout their conversation by a contention in complimentary exaggeration, arrives effortlessly now, as they confess to an artificial inflation of sentiment, and agree to abandon it. *Exeunt*, says the text. 'Chuckling', I'd be inclined to add.

*

It is an *entente cordiale*, however, which their two principals, the Kings Leontes and Polixenes, have yet to arrive at—which, indeed, they are destined never to achieve. The questioning of *their* hospitable fictions produces no relaxation into laughter, only stubbornness (in Leontes) and discomfort (in Polixenes). The stakes, it seems, have been raised to a level where the game can only be played in deadly earnest. But what is it that's at stake for the Kings, which was not at stake for their servants?

In the Fifteenth Book of the *Odyssey*, Odysseus' son, scouring Greece for his lost father, is being hospitably detained by Menelaus. Like Polixenes, Telemachus is questioned by his fears of what may chance or breed upon his absence. He has left no custodian in charge of his property and has been warned by Athene that 'sneaping winds' may easily blow at home. He doesn't, however, insist on this spur to departure, but appeals broadly to the generosity of his host:

'Sire,' he said, 'I beg leave of you now to return to my own country, for I find myself longing to be home.'

And he meets, in Menelaus, a most un-Leontean tact:

'Telemachus,' the warrior king replied, 'far be it from me to keep you here for any length of time, if you wish to get back. I condemn any host who is either too kind or not kind enough. There should be moderation in all things, and it is equally offensive to speed a guest who would like to stay and to detain one who is anxious to leave …

'However, do give me time to bring you some presents and pack them in your chariot—they will be fine ones, as you will see for yourself. And let me tell the women to get a meal ready in the hall …'
(Homer, *Odyssey*, trans. E. V. Rieu, Penguin edn, 1946, pp. 238–9)

The warmth of Menelaus' welcome is not impugned by his readiness to part warmly; it is confirmed by it. He cares more for the guest's peace of mind than for the triumph of his own benevolence. Once he's satisfied that it isn't some over-polite scruple of 'tiring his royalty' that hastens Telemachus away, he presses him no farther. The boy clearly longs to be home. To detain him now would be 'offensive'.

Leontes feels no such scruple. He seems to take umbrage at the mere hint of departure. His overbearing manner may contain some rough affection, but it certainly doesn't treat Polixenes' longing for home as meriting serious consideration:

>   Stay your thanks a while,
>   And pay them when you part.
> Pol.   Sir, that's tomorrow.
>   I am question'd by my fears of what may
>   chance
>   Or breed upon our absence, that may blow
>   No sneaping winds at home, to make us say
>   'This is put forth too truly.' Besides, I have
>   stay'd
>   To tire your royalty.
> Leon.   We are tougher, brother,
>   Than you can put us to't.
> Pol.   No longer stay.
> Leon.   One sev'night longer.
> Pol.   Very sooth, tomorrow.
> Leon.   We'll part the time between's then; and in that
>   I'll no gainsaying.
>
>   (I.ii. 9)

There's no doubt that this plays best if it's handled jocularly. It could so easily be purely good-humoured—a little two-handed comedy of intransigence by which two friends act out the reluctance they feel at parting. But don't we also hear in Leontes' bearish gruffness an over-surfeited conviviality—as if the more he senses his own *in*hospitable weariness, the less able he is to admit it? Under this browbeating, at all events, Polixenes' tone becomes faintly harassed, as if (to put what is merely a glimpsed possibility, as a proposition) he is being forced to put their 'rooted affection' to a test that makes him unhappy:

Press me not, beseech you, so.
There is no tongue that moves, none, none i'th'world, So
soon as yours could win me.

(I.ii. 19)

But there is, of course, one such tongue, and we are
shortly to hear it 'win' him with effortless ease. The
intransigence, apparently, is not about the request but the
requester. And we are also, at this point, being alerted to
something overbearing in Leontes' way of loving people—
something which elicits these protestations-in-resistance
from those who are close to him. In a minute, we are to hear
a similar note from Hermione:

—Yet, good deed, Leontes,
I love thee not a jar o'th'clock behind
What lady she her lord.

(I.ii. 42)

You do not say such things to a man who is secure in his own
sufficiency. Something unhappy haunts these assurances of
affection, as if the speaker fears to be unbelieved—as,
indeed, when once the assurances become necessary, there
is a good chance she (or he) will be. But that is for the future.
For the moment it remains a subliminal flicker of
perception.

I have foregrounded this very 'social' embarrassment that
the two Kings find themselves in, even at the risk of over-
emphasis, because it may just be one of the 'conditions' of
what 'happens' to Leontes. On one level it's a perfectly
commonplace thing, a familiar foolish tussle of wills over a
matter of small importance. Anyone who has paid an
extended visit knows that it's easy to overshoot the right
time for leaving and that, once that time has passed, it may
be difficult to extricate yourself without offence. Both
parties having now become committed to an exaggerated
version of their cordiality, the admission by either that it is
so, puts both of them in the wrong.

Polixenes plainly longs for the salt air and the open
seaways that lead to home. His brother's love has become a
'whip' to him (I.i. 25). The hospitality may be 'freely given',
but he's not feeling it that way any more:

> Time as long again
> Would be fill'd up, my brother, with our thanks,
> And yet we should for perpetuity
> Go hence in debt.
>
>   (I.ii. 3)

He is labouring under an unwieldy burden of obligation
which seems to crush all remaining pleasure out of the visit.
But he can't say so, any more than Leontes can say, 'Go, if
you must. But I wish you wouldn't'. Instead, Polixenes spins
excuses (cares of state), which are promptly rebutted (only
the bygone day he had satisfaction on that score: I.i. 31), fails
to take up the 'strong' reason Hermione proffers him (that
he 'longs to see his son'), and is driven finally to the
embarrassed insincerity of fearing to be 'a charge and
trouble' to them—as if that could ever be an issue between
real friends!

Real friends, though? Isn't that, with the dismal escalation
of small misunderstandings into great, becoming precisely
the question? Leontes seems to think so. That is why the
friendship has to be 'proved' by the pointless extra
'sev'night'. Perhaps it is also why, for the forty-odd lines
that Hermione undertakes his pleading for him, he walks
out on the conversation so completely that he has to inquire
about its outcome. Perhaps that is why, having had a
consent wrung for him, his first blurted reaction is one of
resentment at the previous denial—'At *my* request he would
not' (editors have no warrant for marking this as an *Aside*:
its awkward clumsiness is there for everyone to hear). All
this is the behaviour of a man plagued with a mistrust that he
cannot admit to consciousness, and which he must
therefore blame on someone else. 'You don't really love me

at all', is the accusation we level against the person we're beginning to cease loving ourselves.

Some readers have found it very puzzling that Leontes is so ready to suspect his dearest friend of the ultimate betrayal, as if Polixenes were no nearer an acquaintance, and no better known to him than 'Sir Smile his neighbour'. But perhaps, as is not impossible with dearest friends, he *is* no better known. For decades, their encounters have all been by attorney—'with interchange of gifts, letters, loving embassies', as Camillo tells us (I.i. 25). In these years of separation they have traversed the critical years between puberty and manhood; they have grown up, married, had children, and assumed the government of their countries. The wide gap of time that has dissevered them will be hard to close. Hard, but not impossible, provided the gap is recognised, and their 'more mature dignities and royal necessities' form the basis of a re-established intimacy.

But this is a play about interrupted continuities; about gaps that remain unfilled by natural growth and maturation; about ruptured developmental bonds; about sixteen frozen years of fruitless penitence, and about equally frozen idealities which will tyrannise permanently over a budding nature, if 'dear life' does not redeem them.

Furthermore, natural growth and maturation is exactly what Polixenes, for one, finds it impossible to envisage. Nothing, for him, can bridge the gap between boyhood and manhood, because he has made the boy in himself nostalgically 'eternal', and he himself wanders like a phantom of regret in the lost green fields of youth. The processes that have intervened he mentions only to deplore. He is a man who demands that Time stand still, knowing that it won't. And we see him holding out this golden dream, to himself and to Hermione, while the man he is supposed to share it with, sullen as a rebuffed schoolboy, mooches about the stage or plays desultorily with his son, out of earshot and apparently careless of the outcome.

There *are* two boys eternal on stage, suffering, both of

them, with all the child's capacity to be hurt and not to understand. But lamblike they are not!

I don't mean to be snide at these men's expense. The eternal child survives in all of us. It is the very quick of growth and change and hope. But a child must play. It needs to be able to giggle at its own absurdities—as we saw Camillo and Archidamus doing. It needs to be able to long irrationally for home, and be unashamed of it; to wish desperately that the friend would stay, but let him go if he wants. A child can be vulnerable without feeling humiliated. But the childness in these two Kings, obliquely reflected in their unusual attachment to their own children, is not the 'varying childness' Polixenes cherishes in his son—the childness that cures 'thoughts that would thick my blood'. It has none of that spontaneous mutability. It has lost the capacity to *play*. The very word has become hideous with treacherous double meanings. To 'play' is to sin.

Shakespeare lays out for us the peculiar notion of maturation—the theology of it, almost—that has brought them to this pass:

> We were as twinn'd lambs that did frisk i'th'sun
> And bleat the one at th'other. What we chang'd
> Was innocence for innocence; we knew not
> The doctrine of ill-doing, nor dream'd
> That any did. Had we pursu'd that life,
> And our weak spirits ne'er been higher rear'd
> With stronger blood, we should have answer'd heaven
> Boldly 'not guilty', the imposition clear'd
> Hereditary ours.
>
> (I.ii. 67)

So Polixenes.

That incorruptible critic and austere Jansenist, James Smith, points out what a heterodox brand of Christianity this is (J. Smith, *Shakespearian and Other Essays*, 1974, pp. 145–6): Polixenes speaks as if Original Sin were

somehow avoidable! Smith is right. But more interesting is
the way Polixenes further equates the birth of sin with the
advent of sex ('stronger blood'). Perhaps, listening to
Hermione's charming persuasions and with an eye on the
restless Leontes, he has already had a premonition of the
dismal metamorphosis that can turn three friends into a
triangle. Is he not already too susceptible to her
womanliness? It seems to be beginning. He searches for a
cause. What is it that went wrong? and when? Significantly,
he doesn't examine the present situation. There's no need.
He knows all too well the root of the evil. For Polixenes (in a
pattern familiar to readers of Blake) the Fall is to be dated
from puberty. The snake in the paradise is simply sex.

Hermione had started this train of thought with the
kindliest of intentions. Hoping perhaps to soften her
husband's graceless withdrawal from the conversation, she
had proposed, as a happier topic, Childhood:

> Come, I'll question you
> Of my lord's tricks and yours when you were boys.
> (I.ii. 60)

(understood: 'still quirky enough, in all conscience ... but
never mind'?)

> You were pretty lordings then!

But the topic is far from happy, charged with regret and guilt
as it is; and her own warm presence makes it even less
happy. The boy Polixenes feels profoundly threatened in
this region of memory.

It's a strange enough boyhood that the King of Bohemia
projects: lambs frisking in the sun is not the image most
naturally suggested by the yelling hordes in a primary school
playground. But it's an even stranger notion of maturation:
one grows up only to learn 'the doctrine of ill-doing', to be
reared with 'stronger blood' which is, apparently, vicious in

its effects. As strange, certainly, it strikes Hermione, to judge
by her slightly impish primness in reply:

> By this we gather
> You have tripp'd since. (I.ii. 75)

Hermione knows the regions of experience Polixenes
gestures towards, but *her* word for them is 'tripp'd'. The 'ill-
doing', 'guilt', and 'stronger blood' do not touch her, except
to amuse by their blundering intensity. But Polixenes, quite
deaf to the light rebuke, blunders on in, right up to his ears.
Now we discover what it is about the 'stronger blood' that
so alarms him:

> O my most sacred Lady
> Temptations have since then been born to's, for
> In those unfledg'd days was my wife a girl;

(you can almost hear Hermione's jaw drop in amazement;
but there is better to come)

> Your precious self had then not cross'd the eyes
> Of my young playfellow.
>
> (I.ii. 76)

'Grace to boot!' interrupts Hermione, torn between
incredulity and laughter,

> Of this make no conclusion, lest you say
> Your queen and I are devils.
>
> (I.ii. 80)

If Polixenes doesn't blush at this point, he's thicker-skinned
than I take him to be. This was, infallibly, the 'conclusion'
he was about to make; and the moral disarray that has him
call his hostess, in one breath, both 'sacred' *and*
'temptation' is profoundly revealing.

But Hermione takes mercy on him, deftly diverts the blow and tries to help him out of his absurdity. She has to treat him like the boy he says he wishes he was:

> Yet, go on;
> Th'offences we have made you do we'll answer,
> If you first sinn'd with us, and that with us
> You did continue fault, and that you slipp'd not
> With any but with us.

(I.ii. 82)

She employs his vocabulary of 'offences', 'fault' and 'sinning', but the words are enclosed in audible quotation-marks and mocked by her own word, 'slipp'd'. And the sentiments are bathed in an unmistakable sensuous glow of one who can only hope that such happy faults, so begun, will 'continue'—and 'with us'. Her moral world is leagues away from Polixenes'.

I would not, however, trust Polixenes to hear the quotation-marks or to relish the glow. The guilt-culture of puritanism is not renowned for its responsiveness to humour. Nor is Leontes' sense of humour in much better fettle either. And it is exactly on this note that he rejoins them. We shall never know if Shakespeare meant him to overhear and misconstrue her words, but he easily might. It could explain his choice of a potentially bitter verb: 'Is he *won* yet?'

'He'll stay, my lord', says Hermione, still in the backwash of her own kindly amusement at Polixenes (and therefore not noticing the tone?). Leontes' next remark, however, signalling deeper trouble, cannot and does not escape her— 'At my request he would not.'

I've already indicated the kind of Polixenes-oriented trouble it contains. But it is also unquietly directed at Hermione's unnatural powers of persuasion, and she has heard it. So, with a mixture of tact and urgency she directs the conversation away from both suspicions, onto a ground

of confidence, as she hopes, for all three—reminding
Leontes that they are husband and wife, irrevocably bound,
and choosing to be so.

Here, with his usual consummate unobtrusiveness,
Shakespeare is giving us the long perspective on this
particular marriage and its origins. And he's doing so
because this too has contributed to the unique situation—
this and no other—in which the nightmare that comes upon
Leontes has its own logic.

Their courtship, we learn, had some special vicissitudes:

> Three crabbed months had sour'd themselves to death,
> Ere I could make thee open thy white hand
> And clap thyself my love; then didst thou utter
> 'I am yours for ever.'
>
> (I.ii. 102)

Three months, some annotators say, was long for an
Elizabethan courtship, and especially long for a marriage
that was dynastic in origin, between a king and an emperor's
daughter. It doesn't matter. It *felt* long to Leontes: its length
is still 'sour' in memory. But of course the Hermione we see
is exactly the woman to refuse to have her judgement
hustled. The white hand opens only when the candid mind
consents. She wants the words 'for ever' to mean what they
say. And conversely, the Leontes we see is exactly the man
to feel this delay as 'crabbed', a slur upon his sufficiency, and
to be unable to grasp the importance, for a Hermione, of a
clear resolution.

All marriages carry the stamp of the conditions under
which they were contracted. They will crack at the point
where they were least firmly cemented. And all marriages
have an array of inequalities built into their mutuality. But
the inequalities of this marriage are of the radical kind that
may distil slow gall. The sourness lives on. Leontes speaks
of the crabbed months with no softening suggestion that
they have passed quietly into history. And that, too, is

understandable—for Hermione, throughout this scene and beyond, seems in possession of an elasticity and largeness, a free 'play' of spirit which he cannot command and cannot rise to. It would be hard not to resent it, somewhere.

But the speech must go back into its context. For the *way* the recollection arises is just as important as the *fact* that it arises. Recovering from the grumpiness of 'At my request he would not', Leontes has tried to make amends:

> Hermione, my dearest, thou never spok'st
> To better purpose.
>
> (I.ii. 88)

This could, of course, bear a very bitter construction: something along the lines of, 'You imagine yourself to be invisible in your "purpose", but "you'll be found,/Be you beneath the sky."' Something in the tone, at all events, elicits a sharp note of interrogation from Hermione, as if her ear has caught an echo of inner disquiet. 'Never?' she queries, looking him keenly in the eye.

He would not appear to be meeting the eye. Though he must know her meaning, he's strangely recalcitrant in acknowledging it, muttering,

> 'Never but once.'

They are now in very deep waters. There can be no mystery about the other 'once', but for Polixenes' sake at least, the tone must be lightened to include an observer of these intimacies. That's probably why Hermione begins almost archly, teasingly—

> What! Have I twice said well? When was't before?
> I prithee tell me—
>
> (I.ii. 90)

But she very quickly finds herself slipping into a bantering levity which can only make matters worse. And though she stops half-a-dozen times in hopeful expectation, Leontes will not rescue her. The 'once before' has become as impossible for him to name as she is determined to make him name it.

It plays unhappy tricks with her tone. He cannot know that what reaches him as provocative femininity deliberately flaunting itself before another male—

> you may ride's
> With one soft kiss a thousand furlongs ere
> With spur we heat an acre,
>
> (I.ii. 94)

and so on—is just a woman discovering distressfully that *anything* she says is going to be received on the level of sexual provocation. The very foreignness of guilt to her temperament will make her sound 'loose' to guilty ears. Or, as she puts it at her trial,

> Mine integrity
> Being counted falsehood shall, as I express it,
> Be so received.
>
> (III.ii. 34)

Her life already stands in the level of his dreams. Her words have passed out of her control, subject to the nightmare metamorphosis that suspicion can always impose on them.

She tries to arrest that miserable momentum, valiantly cheerful, but her cajolery, repelled, takes on a tone that is almost silly:

> My last good deed was to entreat his stay;

(Polixenes, notice, is now completely out of account—a mere parenthic 'him')

What was my first? It has an elder sister,
Or I mistake you. O, would her name were Grace!
But once before I spoke to th'purpose—When?
Nay, let me have't; I long.

(I.ii. 97)

Now Leontes must reply, wretched with misgiving though
he is, and name the occasion which ought to be the root and
ground of sunny confidence. But there can be no sunny
confidence in what *he* remembers, only deeper misgiving—
crabbed months souring themselves to death, the white
hand reluctantly opening:

> then didst thou utter
'I am yours for ever.'

(I.ii. 104)

That is the knife-edge. It can be the ceremony by which
the bond is reconsecrated, as Hermione again opens her
hand to receive his, breathing ''Tis Grace indeed' with a
sober fervency from which all the silliness has vanished, and
which registers immense relief, I think, at being clear of the
minefields of mistrust. She was right! It was just one of those
fantasms that can cloud the clearest vision; and by treating it
as if it didn't exist she has exorcised it.

But Leontes' words have another resonance, a
questioning, probing, unhappy one—'*then* didst thou
utter/"I am yours for ever"', but now ...? In the light of
those crabbed months, were you concealing something?
And are you now repenting? Can thy dam ... may't be ...
affection? He is on the brink of committing himself to that
hideous vision, at exactly the same moment as he struggles
to affirm his trust in their mutual vows.

If Hermione hears that in his words, she hears it only to
discount it as ignoble—ignoble in him, as it would be
ignoble in her to respond to it. The response could only
look like guilt, and does not become a lady like her. If he has

put her in the false, ludicrous position of choosing between
her husband and her husband's friend, she will show her
superiority to the suspicion, by seeming unaware of its very
possibility. He has placed his hand in hers again. She will use
her renewed power over him to place her other hand in
Polixenes' ... and unite them, after the pitiful, trivial,
transient cloud that has passed between them. Instead of
being the cause of division, she will be the instrument of
reconciliation.

It's an act of high courage, expressing the perilous extent
of her trust in Leontes' wholesome integrity. Equally it is an
act of folly. She cannot know it perhaps, but it is fatally
miscalculated in its very eloquence:

> Why, lo you now, I have spoke to th'purpose twice:
> The one for ever earn'd a royal husband;
> Th'other for some while a friend.

(I.ii. 106)

With a gracious smile for Polixenes, she stresses the
antithesis between the 'for ever' of marriage and the 'some
while' of friendship. But Leontes is already gone. The word
he hears is 'friend'. It's a neutral word which, like a lot of
other innocent words (such as 'play' or 'neat' or 'love' or
'satisfy'), *must* be used, because there is no other. But it
reaches his ears as an obscene euphemism.

He lets the hand fall, resuming his restless pacings, toying
fretfully with the bewildered Mamillius; and everything that
is to follow is already there, fully formed—'Too hot, too
hot!' He has given himself up to the foul, familiar
imaginings—gone rag-picking among the ancient garbage of
misogynist cynicism and misanthropic prurience, and the
momentum of that will carry him far—past, even, the
categorical denial of Apollo—before it is exhausted. The
momentum is given us in the rhythms and cadences of his
speech:

Too hot, too hot!
To mingle friendship far, is mingling bloods.
I have tremor cordis on me: my heart dances.
But not for joy; not joy.

                    (I.ii. 108, Folio punctuation)

Yet one hears, potently, how, in its own demonic way, it *is* a kind of joy—a frenzied stimulation of the nerves and the blood, beside which everything else comes to seem pallid, insipid, and implausible.

It is also self-confirming in a thoroughly deadly way. By letting go the hand that gave her heart to him, Leontes leaves Hermione holding only ... the hand of Polixenes—an action which, of necessity, must next be translated as 'paddling palms and pinching fingers'. By the withdrawal of his hand, the breach of his trust, he has *made* it that. And Hermione has no redress. She cannot change her behaviour in the light of his guilty suspicion without becoming contaminated by it. It is the same merciless principle of integrity that is enunciated in *Macbeth*:

Though all things foul would wear the brows of grace,
Yet grace must still look so.

It's open to us in the audience to wonder—when she has *noticed* that her husband 'holds a brow of much distraction'—whether Hermione is well advised to obey his request and go off into the garden arm-in-arm with Polixenes. Yet how could she refuse, since 'grace must still look so'? To change under suspicion is to license the suspicion. There is no integrity so strong that it can dictate its own interpretation. The drama is in motion.

*

I don't know whether Leontes' jealousy still seems 'notoriously unmotivated'. I would have thought that there is rather a profusion of explanations, than a scarcity of them. And they could be very easily multiplied. I might

mention the curious freaks of feeling to which husbands are
sometimes subject in the latter stages of pregnancy—
especially husbands as emotionally centred upon hearth and
home as Leontes seems to be. That is in play here, too. The
parental bond is so essential to this man's stability that he
clutches instinctively at a 7-year-old when he feels himself
falling. Since so much hangs on it, such men are natural
sniffers-out of bastardy. Rather like that idealistic family-
man Leo Tolstoy, there is a passion of domesticity about
Leontes which may easily turn tyrannical. Sixteen years
later, you'll notice, he is *still* speaking of his wife as

> the sweet'st Companion that ere man
Bred his hopes out of, true.
>
> (V.i. 11, Folio text)

In this man's mind, true breeding, hopes, and sweetness are
indissolubly connected. And now to be discarded thence....

But I would not want to lay all the stress on psychological
idiosyncrasy, meticulously though it is charted in the text.
That would be to make it too much of a special case, and to
lose the essential and archetypal from the tale. For there is a
sense in which, the moment Leontes starts drawing water
from the poisoned wells of his prurience, there is no need
for explanation at all. Harold Goddard offers an
illuminating comparison. 'Leontes' jealousy of Polixenes',
he writes,

> is like Shylock's hatred of Antonio (and Shakespeare uses
the same two metaphors of wind and waves to convey it).
In that case nothing personal, but centuries of
mistreatment of the Jews, was the 'motive.' In this case
nothing personal, but the whole history and inheritance
of human jealousy, is the cause. What we are dealing with
here is nature in the raw, with the fantasy-making of the
unconscious mind and the emotional fury it engenders.
Leontes' mind is like a fiery furnace at such a temperature

that everything introduced into it—combustible or not—
becomes fuel. That he threatens in turn to have his wife,
the child, and Paulina *burned* is significant repetition and
detail that indicate the volcanic depth from which his
passion comes.

(H. C. Goddard, *The Meaning of Shakespeare*, 1960, II,
p. 266)

There is a realm of experience—and Shakespeare knew it
well—where 'nothing is but what is not'. It is something
more than delusion. Enter it, and your 'single state of man'
will be shaken by a 'phantasma and a hideous dream' which
inverts the categories of reality. The mind begins to feed
itself upon the fascination that lies at the shadowed centre of
abhorrence itself. Nor can it easily be prised loose. If a well-
intentioned friend, like Camillo, questions the new
categories, you are furious, and on behalf of *reality*!

       is this nothing?
Why, then the world and all that's in't is nothing;
The covering sky is nothing; Bohemia nothing;
My wife is nothing; nor nothing have these nothings,
If this be nothing.   (I.ii. 292)

'Nothing'—though a pure vacancy of matter—can
nevertheless, like a vacuum, suck reality into itself. It even
has a supra-reality of its own. It brings a dizzying sensation
of initiation, this 'diseased opinion'. And Leontes (there's
no mistaking it) has been infecting his brains with this
hallucinogen. He is able, consequently, to give a classic
description of its pathology:

Affection! thy intention stabs the centre.
Thou dost make possible things not so held,
Communicat'st with dreams—how can this be?—
With what's unreal thou coactive art,
And fellow'st nothing.   (I.ii. 137)

Leontes has here formulated the straining apart of
contradictory sensation that threw Othello into an epileptic
fit. The reason perhaps that *he* does not fall down and foam
at the mouth, is that he has located and begun to relish the
pleasure that even this self-appointed vexation contains.

Yes, I do mean 'pleasure'. Nobody embarks on a course
of gratuitous self-torment without promising himself some
perverse satisfactions along the way. And as Leontes thrusts
Mamillius away to 'Go play', he is clearing a space in which
he can more freely 'play', himself. The need to do so is so
powerful that it will out, even in so mangled a form as this:

> Go play (boy) play, there have been
> (Or I am much deceiv'd) cuckolds ere now,
> And many a man there is (even at this present,
> Now, while I speak this) holds his wife by th'arm
> That little thinks she has been sluic'd in's absence,
> And his pond fish'd by his next neighbour (by
> Sir Smile, his neighbour): Nay, there's comfort in't,
> Whiles other men have gates, and those gates open'd
> (As mine) against their will. Should all despair
> That have revolted wives, the tenth of mankind
> Would hang themselves. Physic for't there's none:
> It is a bawdy planet, that will strike
> Where 'tis predominant; and 'tis pow'rful: think it:
> From east, west, north, and south, be it concluded,
> No barricado for a belly. Know't,
> It will let in and out the Enemy,
> With bag and baggage ...
>
> (I.ii. 187, Folio punctuation)

The extraordinary rhythms of this, slipshod and angry-
sulky, remind one of a sullen and ostracised child kicking at
tussocks in the corner of the playground.

Nor is Shakespeare the playwright to forget—now, while
he speaks this—the citizens who have brought their wives to
the playhouse, or the gallants placing themselves

strategically to catch the eye of those wives. And I daresay, as Leontes picked his grim way through the grimier alleys of his own mind, there was a citizen or two who found his grip on his wife's arm involuntarily tightening, and his eyes flitting helplessly towards his next (smiling) neighbour. The instinct touched is very primitive and very powerful. The sentiments, in a sense, require no explanation at all. They rise from a perennial stratum of the male mind, and one which (I think this is the impression conveyed by Leontes' tone of gloomy relish), one which has been made familiar by much frequentation. The frequentation is recorded in words like 'Inch-thick', 'fork'd', 'sluic'd', 'fish'd', 'bawdy', and in the whole swaggeringly hard-bitten manner ('think it!' 'know't!' 'Be it concluded!'), which seems, utterly incongruously, to have a ring of gratified exultation about it: 'Physic for't there's none'—as if the thing that torments him is also a source of unholy jubilation. 'Nay, there's comfort in't' has an irony beyond the fact that the fellowship of cuckolds would seem to provide scant 'comfort' for poor Leontes. The darker irony is that the comfort he is discovering is real and deep.

Just as the luxury of schizoid states can provide a real solvent for problems that are impervious to sanity, so jealousy consoles the man who believes himself to be merely its victim. And in Leontes' unleashed fantasy, Shakespeare has tapped the region of the psyche where we are all accessible to that satisfaction-in-revulsion, the grim exultation of the unsurprised cynic in a bawdy world. Perhaps it's even misleading to call it a region of the psyche at all, implying some dark under-consciousness. Rather, by an imperceptible jar to the perceptive faculties, all that is natural and pleasing and delightful in one's sexual nature becomes lurid with lasciviousness—yet not just lurid, also thrilling as no natural sensuality could ever be. Pleasure with the additional edge that's put upon it by believing it sin. And the self-appointed victim will feed his imagination with the picture of someone he loves committing the hideousness, rather than forgo the rapture of imagining it:

> Is whispering nothing?
> Is leaning cheek to cheek? Is meeting noses?
>   [Folio: 'meating']
> Kissing with inside lip? Stopping the career
> Of laughter with a sigh?—a note infallible
> Of breaking honesty. Horsing foot on foot?
> Skulking in corners? Wishing clocks more swift ...
>   (I.ii. 283)

I don't think the swiftness of events here allows us time to inquire *how* Leontes has become so inward with the gradations of breaking honesty (certainly not by watching Hermione); but the inwardness of the knowledge is striking to the ear.

So when he demands angrily,

> Dost think I am so muddy, so unsettled,
> To appoint myself in this vexation; sully
> The purity and whiteness of my sheets—
> Which to preserve is sleep, which being spotted
> Is goads, thorns, nettles, tails of wasps ...
> Without ripe moving to't? Would I do this?
>   (I.ii. 325)

without for one moment questioning the reality of his anguish (there in the uncontrolled association of sheets, spots, goads, thorns, tails—as if sexuality itself were torment and pollution), one can still reply, 'Yes, you would do this! And that is not so strange as you think. Men *do* appoint themselves in this vexation, especially when they are already feeling muddy and unsettled. An Othello does not need his Iago. He can find "ripe moving" enough in the contradictory impulsions of his own nature.'

For jealousy is not a single emotion, but the confluence of many emotions. It doesn't even exclude a passionate wish to be *rescued* from jealousy. And Shakespeare in a masterly way also gives us the poignant wrestlings, the desperate signallings of the jealous man, as he is sucked into the quagmire. When Leontes' frantic behaviour draws the concerned eyes of his wife and his friend—'How is't with you, best brother?'—it isn't a piece of transparent Macbeth-like lying that he offers in excuse ('Give me your favour. My dull brain was wrought/With things forgotten'), but a kind of oblique truth:

> Looking on the lines
> Of my boy's face, methoughts I did recoil
> Twenty-three years; and saw myself unbreech'd,
> In my green velvet coat; my dagger muzzl'd,
> Lest it should bite its master—
>
> (I.ii. 153)

The 'recoil' is vivid as a snapshot, right down to the toy dagger and the remembered garment. What we are hearing is the small, childlike voice of Leontes' embattled sanity. Trying to hold on. Trying to admit, trying to confess and, by confession, to neutralise, naturalise that terrifying recoil upon infantile vulnerability. The dizzying backward slippage across the wide gap of time has terrified him. He is *feeling* like that little green-coated boy—horribly dependent on a love that may not be forthcoming, reduced to childish stratagems, to crude blackmailing appeals for sympathy—like the one that cries out to us from the beginning of this very speech:

> How sometimes nature will betray its folly,
> Its tenderness, and make itself a pastime
> To harder bosoms!
>
> (I.ii. 151)

The catch in the voice ('its folly,/Its tenderness') is almost tearful. It affects jocularity, but it is crying at the same time,

'Save me, rescue me, mother me! Don't turn that adult
imperviousness of the hard bosom on my "tenderness"!'
Leontes *wants* to be found out, and stopped, quite as
much as he craftily evades detection:

>   My brother,
> Are you so fond of your young prince as we
> Do seem to be of ours?

(I.ii. 163)

('I only "seem" to be fond, you see: my bosom is as hard as
the next man's. And God knows whose bastard he mightn't
be, if the truth were out. But if you're very smart you'll see
that I only *seem* to be talking of this matter, because the
other ... the other is unspeakable.')
And there is one last desperate throwing of himself upon
Hermione's percipience, in the strangled unavowable
torment of,

>   Hermione,
> How thou lov'st us show in our brother's welcome;
> Let what is dear in Sicily be cheap.

And I don't see why we need disbelieve him, when he adds,

> Next to thyself and my young rover, he's
> Apparent to my heart.

(I.ii. 173)

That's another grab at normality—if only it will hold. But
the chuckling devil of equivocation picks his fingers loose:
the Polixenes who is 'apparent' is not just the heir apparent
to his love, but the one who is manifest, unmasked, exposed
at his dirty work of betrayal. Leontes, probably, no longer
knows which he meant; but there is no mistaking which
angel it is that now has his ear:

> I am angling now,
> Though you perceive me not how I give line.
>
> (I.ii. 180)

He has identified himself, fully and finally, with the Tempter who, along with other damned souls, angles in the lake of darkness.

*

That's as far as I need go, I think.

Leontes' jealousy is not 'causeless', any more than it is justified. It is both helplessly involuntary *and* it is recklessly chosen. In the ensuing set-to with Camillo it is unmistakable that he only shallowly believes his own suspicion, that it is all a kind of diabolically wilful game. Contradicted, he can manage only petulance:

> It is; you lie, you lie.
> I say thou liest, Camillo, and I hate thee;
> Pronounce thee a gross lout, a mindless slave ...
>
> (I.ii. 199)

That is the peevish vehemence of the playground, which confirms its obstinacy by abusive repetition and has no interest in the truth. And yet we have also experienced, in the mesmeric violence of his utterances, the force of the current that has carried him away.

One only finds all this inexplicable, causeless, 'unmotivated', if one seeks explanation on too naïve a level. The objection to 'psychologising' (as so often) turns out to be simply an objection to crude psychology. To see how unconstrainedly the action accords with the known human heart and mind, is to free ourselves to grasp its huge importance.

An analogy may help. In Conrad's *Chance*, Marlow is reflecting on the tension of a false sexual situation, between Flora de Barral and Captain Anthony. Here, as in Sicilia,

two potentially wholesome affections have 'branched' so
drastically that they seem unable any longer to 'embrace ...
as it were from the ends of opposed winds'. Marlow
comments,

> Of all the forms offered to us by life it is the one
> demanding a couple to realize it fully, which is the most
> imperative. Pairing off is the fate of mankind. And if two
> beings thrown together, mutually attracted, resist the
> necessity, fail in understanding and voluntarily stop short
> of the—the embrace, in the noblest meaning of the word,
> then they are committing a sin against life, the call of
> which is simple. Perhaps sacred. And the punishment of
> it is an invasion of complexity, a tormenting, forcibly
> tortuous involution of feelings, the deepest form of
> suffering ...
>   (J. Conrad, *Chance*, Part II, Ch. 6, 1949, pp. 426–7)

Out of this suffering, Marlow believes, 'something
significant may come at last'—as it shiningly does in
Conrad's novel, and in Shakespeare's play. The noble
embrace may be achieved and the life-affections satisfied.
But we will understand the process better if we realise that
the tormenting complexity arises from a defiance of
simplicity. Is it possible, Shakespeare is asking at the outset
of his play, that this primal, commonplace, momentous
human imperative will prove stronger in the end than the
tortuously involuted feelings produced out of its thwarting?
Must there be tragedy?

As for the 'mode' of the play ... what is one to say? After
only one Act, it already has so many! Among them,
certainly, we can make out the mythic triumph of
wickedness, the paradigm of fairy tale. But this co-exists
with, and is empowered by, a psychological naturalism of
quite amazing depth and resourcefulness. What 'mode' do
you call that?

The mode of *The Winter's Tale*, perhaps.

· 2 ·

The Good Queen
Acts II and III

There is a long-running critical dispute concerning the first half of *The Winter's Tale*, in which, before I'm through, I shall probably become disgruntledly embroiled: is it 'tragic'? or is it not? At the moment, though, I'd prefer to stave it off with a provisional remark of two. Such as: whatever tragic potential the action contains, the Leontes we have been watching is hardly the stuff tragic heroes are made of. Neither is Polixenes. If there's any tragedy about, it would seem to attach to Hermione—beset as she is by touchy, vacillating, insufficient or wrong-headed men. Even the trusty Camillo, who

> would not be a stander-by to hear
> My sovereign mistress clouded so, without
> My present vengeance taken,
>
> (I.ii. 279)

—even Camillo, when the opportunity presents itself, offers no 'vengeance' and fails even to 'stand by'. For all his solicitude, he leaves his sovereign mistress to her fate. The only man amongst them all, it would seem, is Mamillius.

And indeed, as Paulina pitches into Leontes (and as her husband stands modestly back, letting her 'take the rein'), there's a strong suggestion that it is only amongst the women

31

that any steadfastness, fidelity or courage is to be found.
'Emilia,' (the Queen's faithful attendant) is a name that had
occurred to Shakespeare before in this context; and the
glancing identifications of Paulina with Dame Partlet the hen
and Lady Margery Midwife strengthen the impression of
female solidarity in a weak-male-dominated world. Men
who are so easily 'unroosted' as these, one rather feels,
deserve to be 'woman-tir'd'—or hen-pecked, as we would say
(II.iii. 74–5).

The tone of all this is curious. Though dreadful things are
happening in Act 2 (primarily to Hermione) and though we
are even presented with a full-frontal view of attempted
infanticide, there is an insidious and pervasive comedy of
the sexes in the handling of it all. The treatment of Leontes,
in particular, brings him dangerously close to buffoonery.

Polixenes is perhaps an exception: he is allowed a partial
rehabilitation before his flight. In the hasty confabulation
with Camillo that ends Act 1, his sense of the enormity of
the disaster does him credit, even if his timidity before its
consequences doesn't:

> This jealousy
> Is for a precious creature; as she's rare,
> Must it be great; and as his person's mighty,
> Must it be violent; and as he does conceive
> He is dishonour'd by a man who ever
> Profess'd to him, why, his revenges must
> In that be made more bitter.
>
> (I.ii. 451)

But the thing I find striking about this résumé, with all its
concatenated 'musts', is its tendency to exonerate Leontes.
Far from finding something monstrous in the King's
suspicion, Polixenes thinks it all too intelligible. He, too, is a
male. And it's as if, in meeting the reddened eye of that
jealousy, he is being forced to acknowledge kinship; as if he
races over the sequence of escalating violences with the swift

comprehension of an accomplice. Because this is the way *his*
mind works, he presents it as the way *any* man's mind must
work. As he says, 'Fear o'ershades me'. But it is less a fear of
Leontes' rage against himself, fear of the 'bespic'd cup' and
the 'lasting wink', than a fear of himself, the self he
recognises in Leontes, that sends him packing in such
indecent haste. We may be glad for even that degree of self-
knowledge; but under the overshading wings of the fear,
Hermione gets consigned to a troubled parenthesis:

> Good expedition be my friend, and comfort
> The gracious Queen, part of his theme, but nothing
> Of his ill-ta'en suspicion! Come, Camillo ...
>
> (I.ii. 458)

Camillo regularly receives critical commendations as 'the
Good Counsellor'. But how he and Polixenes can fail to see
that their flight will give to the 'ill-ta'en suspicion' a weight
amounting almost to proof, is really quite stupefying. The
only explanation is that, in their anxiety for their own skins,
they have effectively forgotten the plight of 'the gracious
Queen'. ''Tis safer to/Avoid what's grown than question
how 'tis born.' And so, from that fine and ancient male mess
created by first deifying women as 'precious'/'gracious'/
'sacred', and then treating them as property, the males flee in
confusion. Which is easy for them to do because, of course,
they 'command/The keys of all the posterns'. They leave
Hermione, as it were, holding the baby. Or—if we count
Leontes—the babies.

All of which may sound like post-feminist anachronism.
But the Shakespeare of Sonnet 143 was able to picture
himself as a loudly crying infant, trailing after his mother-
mistress, begging her to 'play the mother's part, kiss me, be
kind'. He was perfectly capable, surely, of noticing such
behaviour in another man.

To Hermione as mother-mistress, at all events, the
husband proves much more of a burden than the daughter

in her womb, or the son at her skirts. Mamillius emerges
with much credit: he really is 'a gallant child'. When, with
the fretfulness of advanced pregnancy, his mother pushes
him away, he goes obediently and plays with the court
ladies, waiting until she's 'for him again'. Then he returns
and tries (gallantly) to entertain her with one of his
'powerful' tales—though one notices the amusing difficulty
as he has in standing still while he tells it: 'Nay, come, sit
down: then on' (like most small boys, Mamillius tends to
narrate on the hoof).

All the intuitive sympathy for Hermione that's lacking in
Leontes, overflows in Mamillius' small heart. The boy is so
innocent of accusation that his father can even misconstrue
his childish misery as chiming with his own:

> To see his nobleness,
> Conceiving the dishonour of his mother.
> He straight declin'd, droop'd, took it deeply,
> Fasten'd, and fix'd the shame on't in himself:
> Threw off his spirit, his appetite, his sleep,
> And downright languish'd.
>
> (II.iii. 12, Folio punctuation)

For all the father's obtuseness about its cause, this
behaviour is poignantly recognisable: a mute anguish of
bewilderment, which will fasten and fix all the shame in
itself rather than accuse those it loves. The irony is
appalling. Mamillius' silent 'languishing' is sparing his
father, amongst other things, the knowledge that he is
conceiving the dishonour of his *father*, not his mother. Not
that the child undertakes to judge between them: all he
knows is that his father wants to kill his mother—from
whom he has been violently snatched, like some pawn in an
incomprehensible game. He fears he will never see her again.
And the 'mere [i.e. unconditional, absolute] conceit and
fear' this inspires is enough to destroy him.

Anyone who thinks the death of Mamillius is another of

Shakespeare's 'plot-postulates' has something to learn
about the grief of children over the rupture of family life.
And the small pathos of his passing is made weightier by the
insensitivity of the 'gross and foolish sire' with which it is
contrasted.

The weight of the indictment that is accumulating against
Leontes is, by now, so crushing that we may wonder how he
can survive at all as an object of serious dramatic interest. He
staggers and stammers under the onslaught of Paulina's
scorn, bandies insults with his courtiers, is reduced to
tweaking their noses and pulling their beards, he fumes and
rages like a cardboard Herod, until it seems that the only
action of which *he* can be the dynamic centre is one that will
raise the participants (as Antigonus remarks)

>   To laughter, as I take it,
> If the good truth were known.   (II.i. 198)

Who can seriously care for such a man? The tragic matter
has been dissipated, by indignity, into shallow farce.

Or would have been, if it weren't for two factors. The first
concerns a primal role which is discernible through all
Leontes' personal follies. A man's predicament can matter
where the man himself does not. Drama, I've been arguing,
naturally deals in the local and the specific of the knowable
human psyche. But it need not stop there. It may also reveal
'the translucence of the General in the Especial'—as
Coleridge puts it, in a classic definition of the symbolic. And
even the Especial of farcical stupidity can have this
translucence. It has it, after all, in the opening scene of *King
Lear*. There, the transcendent folly of Lear's action is back-
lit by another glow: it is not just folly we are witnessing, but
the folly of the Father—of all fathers. And while the old
fool's personality and proceedings command scant respect,
the great primal force of the parental bond that burns and
scorches through him is so vast as to require a theatre almost
cosmic for its accommodation.

In a similar way, the acts of the contemptible, self-deluded, wilful Leontes are giving us the folly of The Husband—a perennial, possibly incurable folly from which none of us who are male can claim exemption (perhaps not even those of us who are female, since it takes two to tango to the jealousy tune). We dare not, consequently, treat it with the contempt that it very possibly deserved. Fear o'ershades us. Touched at that level of panic and emptiness, would we make out any better?

The second factor which rescues the action from contempt is, of course, the presence (and she is quite astonishingly 'present') of Hermione. Harrowed but calm, displaying a kind of serenity in her very anguish, she manages, somehow, to continue caring for Leontes—thus rescuing him narrowly from contempt. She is the good Queen. Paulina is right to insist on the word:

> Good Queen, my lord, good Queen—I say good Queen;
> And would by combat make her good, so were I
> A man, the worst about you.

If anyone deserves to be called 'good' (using the word properly—not abusing it like the knuckle-headed males who imagine a woman can be *made* good by the bawling of challenges and the swashing of buckles), it is Hermione. A good Queen. One of the things Leontes is going to have to learn is the meaning of these simple words: 'good'; 'love'; 'warm'. So Paulina drums the lesson into him: 'I say good Queen'.

Hermione's palpable goodness has proved something of a snare to criticism. Commentators have tended to exclaim raptly, ''Tis Grace indeed!' and then to subside into mindless adoration of a notably theological tinge. The apotheosis of femininity swiftly follows. As we've seen, Hermione suffers this misappropriation quite enough at the hands of other people in the play, without the critics joining in. And incidentally, editors have no business

compounding the offence by giving *grace* a capital 'G'. It's
true that the Folio compositor tends to capitalise every
second noun in his text, and 'grace' is one of them; but that's
no reason for removing all the other capitals, leaving *grace*
enjoying a specious prominence—wearing a halo, as it were.
With a Hermione around, there is no need to signal
transcendence so crudely. We can put 'grace' back into
lower-case, and keep the question of its divine origins
properly fluid.

Not that I want in the least to deny Hermione grace. We
have seen her in Act 1, percipient, tactful, troubled, warm,
making her way carefully through the tangled thickets of
Leontes' misprision and self-doubt towards the honourable
'love' which can include both him and his friend, yet betray
none of her integrity either—

> such a kind of love as might become
> A lady like me.
>
> (III.ii. 62)

That is grace. That is 'rare'—to use another of the play's
favourite value-words. To know that there is a whole gamut
of feelings properly called 'love', which are not rivals and
competitors, but kin to each other, is rare.

Equally rare, in the face of a stunning calumny from one
who should 'best know' otherwise, is this:

> Should a villain say so,
> The most replenish'd villain in the world,
> He were as much more villain; you, my lord,
> Do but mistake.
>
> (II.i. 78)

Integrity usually lies close to obstinacy: you honour your
own truth, like Coriolanus, but at some cost to the truth of
those around you. Not so Hermione. Her integrity has none
of that stiffness. It is wounded, but it does not shrivel into

self-righteousness. Its ear is quick, its eye observant, and its
amour-propre too secure to be suddenly stung into
vituperation. But it is not all charitable self-effacement
either. It has its own exactly measured intransigence, an
austerity of emotion which knows what does and does not
'become' it, and which finds its restraints within itself. This
intransigence, Hermione is perfectly aware, will be open to
misconstruction. But it is a part of her self and she is not
ashamed of it:

> Good my lords,
> I am not prone to weeping, as our sex
> Commonly are—the want of which vain dew
> Perchance shall dry your pities—but I have
> That honourable grief lodg'd here which burns
> Worse than tears drown....
> The King's will be perform'd.
>
> (II.i. 107)

If you're in any doubt about the fine poise of this sincerity,
you need only compare the prickly defensiveness of
Hamlet, when *his* sincerity of grief is questioned and he
claims to 'have that within which passes show':

> Seems, madam! Nay, it is; I know not seems.

To find a voice simultaneously, for the 'honourable grief',
for the outrage she's submitted to, for her personal dignity,
and for the impersonal concern that survives all these ... this
would seem an impossible task. But Hermione,
miraculously, finds it:

> Adieu, my lord.
> I never wish'd to see you sorry; now
> I trust I shall.
>
> (II.i. 122)

That grave measured speech, saddened yet dry-eyed, reproachful without sanctimony, angered without egotism, gives us the whole woman she is—a woman strong enough to *wish* upon her husband the misery to which his deeds have entitled him:

> now
> I trust I shall.

The word 'trust' is very exactly chosen: it is her trust in his better nature which reveals to her the necessity of his sorrow. And with all the impersonal austerity of love, she 'trusts' he will undergo it.

That is 'grace'. And it is far too rich and human a quality to be abandoned to the theologians, indeed, the theologians wouldn't be interested in the word if it didn't have that richness.

You may be wondering how I can feel so secure against 'theologians' when this incarnation of womanly grace is to return as a holy statue and be 'resurrected' by awakened 'faith'. Objection noted. But this is a play which rewards being read forwards, and I propose to defer reading it backwards until the simpler method breaks down. I remain impenitently interested in what 'happens'. After all, it was good enough for Shakespeare's first audience; why shouldn't it be good enough for us?

*

Meanwhile, in prison, Hermione gives birth to a 'poor prisoner'—a clear case, it would seem, of the 'imposition ... Hereditary ours' being entailed upon the infant. But the guilt turns out here to be conditional, not absolute:

> A daughter, and a goodly babe,
> Lusty, and like to live. The Queen receives
> Much comfort in't; says 'My poor prisoner,
> I am as innocent as you.'

> (II.ii. 27)

James Smith, no doubt, would find this heterodox; and I'm sure it is. Hermione doesn't make the orthodox comparison between two sinful inheritors of Adam's guilt—which would give 'You are as innocent as I.' She looks at the child—'The innocent milk in it most innocent mouth'— and, with her characteristic neglect of the categories of guilt, claims parity: 'I am as innocent as you.' The essential depravity of infants has always been a difficult doctrine to impose on the human imagination and Hermione's thought is clearly running in another direction when she takes the baby in her arms and 'receives/Much comfort in't'. She is looking at a creature which, with its very first 'wawl and cry', has answered heaven boldly, 'Not guilty'. It is a sight that fortifies her in her *own* innocence—which is all very natural ... but not very Christian.

No more Christian is Paulina's interpretation of the omen:

> This child was prisoner to the womb, and is
> By law and process of great Nature thence
> Freed and enfranchis'd.
>
> (II.ii. 59)

She's talking, of course, about the child's juridical right to leave a literal prison. But it's one of those utterances that reverberates through the whole play, enunciating a general truth about the phenomenon of birth. The baby is not just released from restraint ('freed'), but given a positive place, as of right, in the human community (*enfranchisement:* 'the incorporating of a man to be free of a Company or Body Politique', as Coke has it [OED, 2a]). A new citizen is set unconditionally on the earth. The slate is wiped clean. Whatever the sins of the fathers, now we begin afresh.

Shakespeare knows all about Original Sin, certainly; he may personally have believed in it, we shall never know; but its writ, it seems, is not to run here. There is a higher court of appeal, that of great nature (or 'Nature', if you prefer—but then we'd better follow Folio consistently and capitalise 'Child' and 'Law' as well—it's the same problem of modernisation as with 'grace').

I don't want to labour the point about Shakespeare's 'naturalism'; but I don't want, either, to ignore the extraordinary resonance of Paulina's pronouncement. Long before the arrival of the cheery amoralist, Autolycus, Shakespeare is preparing the soil in which those daffodils of his begin to peer. He has already made out the red blood reigning (or 'raigning'—the Folio spelling keeps open a happy word-play) in the winter's pale. The tight moralism of sin/fault/guilt is slackening its grip as humanity is enfranchised in that ordinary recurrent miracle—spring, birth, great nature. The entailment and bondage melts away as the merely mental thing it was. Other forces in fact govern the world. Leontes is no more than a jealous tyrant usurping his power. He has no jurisdiction over new life.

He does however have power, alarming power, over this particular instance of new life. And the rest of the First Movement goes on to show the havoc he can still wreak with this limited power. Shakespeare may be vindicating the sovereignty of 'great creating nature', but it's no part of his project to minimise the capacity of *human* nature to thwart and destroy. That would make the demonstration a very shallow affair indeed. Both Hermione and Paulina underestimate that destructive capacity—with results that are nearly fatal to Perdita, that 'Poor thing, condemn'd to loss'.

A lot of people besides Leontes, actually, seem to be involved in doing the condemning. Antigonus, for instance, may not be as pusillanimous as the other lords (or as his wife believes him), but he does nevertheless make rather a fetish of his feudal obligations, faithfully performing a vow that is morally repugnant to him. And though he eases his passage with rationalisations drawn from his dreams, this hardly raises him in our estimation, since we know his conclusion to be mistaken. And Paulina—I don't know how it strikes

other readers?—is surely taking a gigantic risk, which it's not
hers to take, when she trusts to a 'better nature' of which
there has been not one sign, and leaves the baby to Leontes'
tender mercies. In Hermione the project was forgivable: she
hadn't seen the implacable obscene fury of the man who had
been her husband against his own offspring. But Paulina has,
and still she lays down the little bundle, consigning it, for all
she knows, to the furnace its father wants it instantly
consumed in. Her action does have the effect of dramatising
the unthinkableness of the thing Leontes now does, but it
seems pretty foolhardy none the less.

Perhaps such speculations are marginal—mistaking the
'mode'. Certainly, as Antigonus takes *up* the bundle (and it
would have been, of course, no more than that on
Shakespeare's stage) we are not too much afeard. Something
in the air is changing. A web of mythopoeic magic is being
woven and cast over the savagery of the act. A fresh breeze
blows from a new quarter. And there is invisible music,
borne over the waves, perhaps, from 'Delphos'
(Shakespeare's imaginary amalgam of mountain Delphi and
island Delos, a place of delicate climate and sweet air, fertile,
ceremonious, solemn and unearthly):

> Come on, poor babe.
> Some powerful spirit instruct the kites and ravens
> To be thy nurses! Wolves and bears, they say,
> Casting their savageness aside, have done
> Like offices of pity. Sir, be prosperous
> In more than this deed does require! And blessing
> Against this cruelty fight on thy side,
> Poor thing, condemn'd to loss.
>
> (II.iii. 184)

Music it unmistakably is—a mere possibility of feeling
substantiated into harmonious sound. For its validation it
depends upon 'some powerful spirit', for no one can
pretend that nature is necessarily benign to this tune; yet the

powerful spirit is already present in the music of its own utterance.

Antigonus has scarcely departed before the messengers from Delphos are announced, their mouths full of prosperity, and their hearts brimming with the hope of 'something rare' that is about to 'rush to knowledge'. The pace quickens with delectable haste:

> Go; fresh horses.
> And gracious be the issue.   (III.i. 21)

'Issue', Molly Mahood has pointed out, is a rich word here. The 'issue', as Paulina has described it—from its frown, its 'pretty dimples', right down to its 'mould and frame of hand, nail, finger'—is indeed gracious. But we have just seen it nevertheless 'hal'd out to murder'. The whole action is poised between a kind of holy hope—which is, in the end, to make the issue more gracious than we could ever have imagined—and a kind of despairing disgust at Leontes' obscene persistence in his 'weak-hing'd fancy'. The trial must settle it all. We refer ourselves to the oracle.

*

If tragedy involves our feeling, upon the very pulses of life, the possibility that life is not worth the having, then, in the Trial Scene, we touch upon tragedy—Hermione's tragedy:

> For life, I prize it
> As I weigh grief, which I would spare.   (III.ii. 40)

More than any statement could do, the numbing cadence gives us the flatness of her misery. Life is not an unconditional good, to be clutched at any cost. For those who think it is, she feels only a pitying scorn:

> Sir, spare your threats.
> The bug which you would fright me with, I seek.

And she goes on to show how easily, with the removal of a few simple 'comforts', life may become utterly barren:

> To me can life be no commodity.
> The crown and comfort of my life, your favour,
> I do give lost, for I do feel it gone,
> But know not how it went; my second joy
> And first fruits of my body, from his presence
> I am barr'd, like one infectious; my third comfort,
> Starr'd most unluckily, is from my breast—
> The innocent milk in it most innocent mouth—
> Hal'd out to murder; myself on every post
> Proclaim'd a strumpet; with immodest hatred
> The child-bed privilege denied, which 'longs
> To women of all fashion; lastly, hurried
> Here to this place, i'th'open air, before
> I have got strength of limit. Now, my liege,
> Tell me what blessings I have here alive
> That I should fear to die.
>
> (III.ii. 89)

Shakespeare can always write wonderfully for the female voice. Boy-actors notwithstanding, you never mistake his women for men. But I think he never so wonderfully caught the *power* of a woman's voice as here—its capacity to be all feeling and flexibility, yet at the same time implacable as steel. She faces the devastation, in full possession of her faculties, and in full knowledge of her loss, yet without blenching. That is how it is. Life can always be stripped of these things. You feel them gone, yet know not how they went. What can a mere death matter, after that?

And yet, in the authentically tragic way, her contempt of death is giving us, *in extremis*, the value of the life that still persists to scorn it. All the sanctities—the crown and comfort of married love, the physical presence of children, the intimacy of the breast, even the fundamental decencies of social respect—have all been violated; but Hermione's high courage survives to despise the despoiled life they have left her to. It's because she knows what life *can* be worth, that she scorns to prolong it on these terms. 'The value of what was destroyed', as D. W. Harding put it, speaking of Rosenberg's war poetry, has been 'brought into sight only by the destruction' (*Experience into Words*, 1963, p.96).

At this point in the action it is, I believe, unthinkable that there can be any return to an equable domesticity. Hermione has been driven too far out into that comfortless asocial wilderness where the tragic individual makes up his accounts with the life 'which [he] would spare'. Her solitude is final. So is her estrangement. Leontes, suddenly catapulted back into the real world a few minutes later, may talk breathlessly of reconciliation, of 'new-wooing' his Queen. With the weight of obsession lifted from his own heart, facile hope floods over him:

Her heart is but o'ercharg'd; she will recover.

(III.ii. 147)

'*But* o'ercharg'd'!—it shows a terrible ignorance of the human heart in general, and of Hermione's in particular! Mamillius' heart, too, was 'but o'ercharg'd.' But we in the audience can hardly countenance his programme of reparation. His situation is like the one that Clytemnestra holds out for Agamemnon's contemplation, as he resolves upon the sacrifice of his daughter Iphigenia:

When you return at last
To Argos, after the war, will you embrace
And kiss your daughters and your son? God forbid!
It would be sacrilege. For do you suppose
Any child of yours, when you have sent
A sister to her death, would ever look
Upon your face again, or in your eyes?

(Euripides, *Iphigenia in Aulis*, trans. C. R. Walker, 1958,
1.1191)

Or any wife? we might add. No. God forbid! It would be sacrilege.

The point is worth making strongly, so that the magnitude of the task Shakespeare has set himself will be manifest. For, although the audience is being given no inkling of it here, he *is* planning a 'return' for his Agamemnon—and not to the butchering and avenging axe of the outraged mother. The temerity of it is staggering. The scheme would seem doomed to disaster—an outrage upon both probability and justice.

Stripped of the continuities of her life—her marriage and her children—Hermione does, however, keep her hold on one or two impersonal continuities which may survive the wreck. As always, her vision extends beyond the vortex into which she is being personally sucked.

She is concerned, firstly, for her honour—not out of vanity, but because

> 'Tis a derivative from me to mine,
> And only that I stand for.   (III.ii. 42)

She knows that the life she prizes 'not a straw' for herself, will nevertheless go on for others. And they must not suffer needlessly. Leontes must be obliged, therefore, to produce better proofs than his jealousies, and to observe law, not rigour. 'Apollo be my judge.'

Nor does she allow her personal catastrophe to draw her into recriminations against the universe at large, as a meaner spirit might have been drawn:

> But thus—if pow'rs divine
> Behold our human actions, as they do,
> I doubt not then but innocence shall make
> False accusation blush.   (III.ii. 26)

Not to doubt at such a moment shows a brave magnanimity,

especially since she holds out to herself no hope of their intervention, only of their beholding. But she has her priorities lucidly clear, and accusing the gods of indifference is not one of them.

And there is one other task she has in hand. It is, if you like, a task of instruction for her obstinate husband, in the matter of Polixenes. He shall not again, if she can help it, confound every important distinction by dividing the integrity of 'love' into two halves, one innocent, the other guilty. Leontes wants to make over her love for his friend, into a 'vice':

> *Leon.*   I ne'er heard yet
> That any of these bolder vices wanted
> Less impudence to gainsay what they did
> Than to perform it first.
> *Herm.*   That's true enough;
> Though 'tis a saying, sir, not due to me.
> *Leon.*   You will not own it.
> *Herm.*   More than mistress of
> Which comes to me in name of fault, I must not
> At all acknowledge.   II.ii. 52)

If boldness signals vice then, yes, she will be vicious in refusing the mere 'name' of vice. But that is not the issue. That is not what she 'stands for'. She stands out here for the proper use of the word 'love', which she knows he wants to deny her. And as (to his mounting fury) she goes on repeating the word in the most vexing of contexts, one can see what her bold intransigence is bent on preserving. It is an essential verity, an emotional truth without which she does not care to have even *his* love:

> For Polixenes,
> With whom I am accus'd, I do confess
> I lov'd him ...

(and her voice rises to bear down the expected objection:
'No, Leontes, you will *not* stop me using the word!')

> ... *lov'd him as in honour he requir'd;*

('I refuse, you see, to set love and honour at odds, as you are
doing.')

> With such a kind of *love* as might become
> A lady like me; with a *love* even such,
> So and no other, as yourself commanded;
> Which not to have done, I think had been in me
> Both disobedience and ingratitude
> To you and toward your friend; whose love ...

('Yes, it is the same word, because it is the same thing')

>   ... whose love had spoke,
> Even since it could speak, from an infant, freely,
> That it was yours.
>   (III.ii. 59)

I find it almost irresistible that the woman who speaks these
lines is discovering that it had been no kindness to cosset
Leontes in his jealous possessiveness, with continual
assurances of love. If they are to have any future relations, it
cannot be on that basis. He must understand that there are
many levels of affection in her nature, all properly called
'love', and, in the name of human dignity, he cannot expect
to monopolise them all. If he knew his own good, he
wouldn't want to. He would value her 'liberty', her
'bounty', her 'fertile bosom' for the generosities of nature
they are. He would see that they *well* become the agent—a
lady like her. And he would be glad that she was such a lady.
   In Act 1 Leontes had glimpsed how these qualities *might*
become her; but, finding them perhaps too hard to live up
to, he took the easier, more squalid course of believing them

to be merely 'a free face *put on*'. Possibly—for their marriage—the instruction now comes too late; but Hermione has decided that, not even for him, will she be any other lady. That is why she puts the stakes so high, why she sets his magnanimity such a searching test: she wants reconciliation at no lower rate.

Leontes seems not to hear her offer. Indeed, he only hears the words of Apollo sufficiently to note that they will not serve his obsession, and then to dismiss them with a casual wave of the hand:

> There is no truth at all i'th'oracle.
> The sessions shall proceed. This is mere falsehood.
>
> (III.ii. 127)

The stunned, incredulous silence into which this falls is broken by the running Servant, and Leontes begins to pay the price of his 'great profaneness'.

*

Except that it isn't he who does the paying. It is Mamillius; and Hermione; and (far away, over on the stormy, bear-encrusted shores of Bohemia) Antigonus. Which is no kind of justice, poetic or otherwise. By its own natural unfolding, the play has generated this new, and very vexing 'problem'. You may say that, for the purposes of the fable, Mamillius and Antigonus no longer 'count'. But they did once; and you can't claim to have solved an equation when you have simply altered the values of some of its terms. Nor can you solve it by wantonly introducing new terms (Autolycus, Perdita, the Shepherds) to which you then assign any value you choose. And the central term, Hermione, lives on, at least in Leontes' memory (if not in Paulina's chapel), with a value quite undiminished, which denies the very possibility of a solution.

In short, there is every sign—and many readers have

taken the signs to be conclusive—that Shakespeare has checkmated himself. He can only gather up the shreds of his tattered fable by beginning all over again, on brand-new premisses: another generation, another country, and, by the way, the wench was *not* dead. And then, really to set the tone, he calls in that old Joker, Time, to warm up the studio-audience, in case they don't laugh in the right places.

That's no way to write a play! Has the old master's hand finally lost its cunning?

· 3 ·

Lead me to These Sorrows
Act III Scene 2

A problem of 'poetic justice' is neither an aesthetic nor a moral matter. It arises when an audience is unable to recognise, in the causal and sequential linkage of the drama, the world they had *thought* they were sharing with the dramatist. And in the wake of that disillusionment they are likely to withdraw their imaginative participation and stand at a farther remove from the action.

With Hermione's 'unjust' death, that kind of strain is put upon the audience. For what kind of a world is it where, without apparent protest, the chief offender can live on, not only unpunished but, in the end, restored and rewarded? It's not so much that we ill-naturedly demand retribution, as that we have some difficulty with a world where it is not exacted.

For the integrity and coherence of what follows, much will depend upon the way Leontes undergoes the sorrow he has so richly earned. And it's just here, it seems to me, that the play runs into a conspicuous difficulty. The difficulty is called Penitence; and it comes to a sharp focus in the person of Paulina, its enforcer.

There are critics who have contrived to defend, even to admire (in a theoretical kind of way) the spiritual therapist that Paulina now—and rather suddenly!—becomes. But I've found none that actually *likes* what she does to her patient.

To be so often resuscitating distress, rubbing the raw spots of memory, to be so regularly unlocking the fountains of his tears, like a penitential water-board official flushing out a hydrant, smacks rather of sadism. 'Why I do trifle thus with his despair', remarks Edgar in an analogous situation, 'is done to cure it'.

I daresay we've all met our Edgars. One of the buzzing aggravations of bereavement is the prompt swarming of the 'curers'—people who know so infallibly what's good for you that they have no leisure to inquire what you actually feel. Edgar's word 'trifle' seems to record some compunction on that score. But if one has any *respect* for the sufferer's despair, more especially if one believes it to be justified (as Leontes' is), one may wonder what possible 'cure' would justify the 'trifling'. I may as well declare myself straight away to be of Cleomines' party, in his dislike of the 'curers' and their methods:

> You might have spoken a thousand things that would
> Have done the time more benefit, and grac'd
> Your kindness better.
>
> (V.i. 21)

He doesn't dispute that Paulina has her own 'kindness'; he would just prefer to see it better 'grac'd'—the 'grace' of courtesy, considerateness, human kindness having become, in Paulina, unhappily antithetical to her (Pauline?) mission of promoting the *other* kind of grace. (Incidentally, if the frequency of quotation and allusion is anything to go by, the Pauline epistles were the books of the Bible that interested Shakespeare least.)

I shall have to postpone a full discussion of the phases of Leontes' penitence, since they are plainest in the last Act. But that is all to the good, because it enables us to watch Leontes as he first embarks upon his sorrows, largely unaided and untutored by the know-alls of the spiritual life. We can try, consequently, to make out the inner logic of his very natural remorse, the momentum and orientation it holds within itself, before it falls into other hands. It's possible, after all, that when Paulina moves in as the director of his penance, she misunderstands and perverts his sorrow. The parallel case of Edgar and Gloucester might at least raise the question.

We go back, then, to the closing moments of the Trial scene (III.ii). We have been shown the strength of Leontes' obsession as it ploughs straight through the flimsy obstruction erected by the oracle. His 'forceful instigation', as he calls it, is as impervious to this as it was to the advice of his lords. Anything that cannot 'relish a truth like us' is by definition 'stupefied'. And then, in a brilliant stroke of drama which is at the same time a profound psychological perception, the whole fabric of his folly collapses.

There is no transition; just an instantaneous reversal. Where he had claimed to 'openly/Proceed in justice', he now talks simply of 'my *injustice*', as if he had always known it for that. The incriminating event he has adduced to demonstrate the flagrancy of Hermione's guilt (the flight of Camillo with Polixenes) now proves Camillo to be 'a man of truth, of mercy'. He speaks as if he has always known the humane and honourable reason that prompted the flight— as indeed he always has. This is not so very strange. The paranoically obsessed mind usually keeps a concealed storage cupboard for the knowledge it boasts to have suppressed: that is just a part of its defensive strategy against surprise attack. And now, when there is nothing left worth defending—the treasure of the citadel, Hermione, being gone forever—he awakes, in plain daylight, from the nightmare, from the 'dream' that Hermione saw levelled at her life, and everything is instantly crystal-clear, not least the blackness of his deeds. He is totally and unaffectedly penetrated with remorse.

The trouble with penitence, however, is that it cannot alter what has been done. It is, in its essence, self-regarding and therefore, in the presence of the larger troubles it has

created, impertinent. A man of any introspection will know
this. Leontes knows it as he bows his head under the fire-
storm of Paulina's indictment. But even that gesture is
impertinent, for it cannot escape the suspicion of
masochistic complacency:

> Go on, go on.
> Thou canst not speak too much; I have deserv'd
> All tongues to talk their bitt'rest.
>
> (III.ii. 211)

It's possible, I think, to find this perfectly just, sincere,
honest ... yet still distasteful. Right at the outset of his
pilgrimage of grief, Leontes seems to be discovering an
ignominious kind of consolation. And it is one, we notice,
which can envisage no change. The condemnation cannot be
spoken too much. It must go on, go on, for ever. And he
must stand forever bowed beneath it.

Near the end of *his* pilgrimage, Lear finds himself trapped
in a similar stasis—though it is one where eternal guilt is
matched with perpetual absolution:

> We two alone will sing like birds i'th'cage;
> When thou dost ask me blessing, I'll kneel down
> And ask of thee forgiveness.

Although this has the warmer colouring imparted by a live
Cordelia, instead of a dead Hermione, it is still piteous—the
frozen tableau of a life that cannot now develop any further.
And Shakespeare mercifully rescues Lear from it, restoring
to him 'the great rage' that makes a man of him again,
bestowing upon him the ineluctable gift of despair and
death.

But Leontes is to enjoy no such restoration to dignity. *He*
cannot kill the slave that was a-hanging Hermione: the slave
was himself. The cleansing anger he might feel becomes
implicated in the masochistic consolations of self-

accusation. There is nothing that, with any decency, he can do, except perhaps what he does next, which is to break down in those helpless sobbings which move even the tough-fibred Paulina:

> Alas, I have show'd too much
> The rashness of a woman! He is touch'd
> To th'noble heart.
>
> (III.ii. 217)

It's a tribute to the three-dimensional depth of Shakespeare's characterisation that we can, even at this late stage, still believe that the heart *is* noble. We have had to deduce the nobility from Hermione's loyalty, or from Paulina's sympathy, but it just survives; and it is able to be consolidated when he refuses the one consolation that is undoubtedly fallacious. Paulina offers it to him:

> What's gone and what's past help
> Should be past grief. Do not receive affliction
> At my petition; I beseech you, rather
> Let me be punish'd that have minded you
> Of what you should forget. Now, good my liege,
> Sir, royal sir, forgive a foolish woman.
>
> (III.ii. 218)

But it is *not* at Paulina's petition that he receives grief. And while it graces her kindness to suggest that *Hermione* is what he 'should forget', he knows better than to believe her. It is a kindness that he must refuse:

> Thou did'st speak but well
> When most the truth; which I receive much better
> Than to be pitied of thee.
>
> (III.ii. 229)

There is precious little manhood left in Leontes, but what

there is speaks here, preferring Truth to Pity. To receive
truth *as* truth, is to escape masochism. And there is one
truth in particular that he is reaching towards. He would
seem to have made out already the loss—not just of
Hermione, but of the Hermione-of-memory—which will
infallibly follow if he admits self-pity or the pity of others,
allowing these to soften or sentimentalise his guilt in the
matter. That is not what he 'should forget', but what he
must remember if he is not to lose her totally. It's a strange
paradox, but one not unknown in the history of grief, that
the wrongs one has done to the beloved dead may become a
bitter jewel in the treasury of memory.

The danger, of course, is that a cult of guilt may grow out
of it whose only consummation can lie in *joining* the beloved
dead. And Leontes' proposals for his future 'recreation'
sound perilously close to a cult of guilt:

> Once a day I'll visit
> The chapel where they lie; and tears shed there
> Shall be my recreation.

(III.ii. 235)

Yet he isn't proposing to fade wispily away into a
necrophiliac revenant: there is some strenuousness in his
resolutions, and some manfulness:

> So long as nature
> Will bear up with this exercise, so long
> I daily vow to use it. Come, and lead me
> To these sorrows.

(III.ii. 237)

That I find moving, though I'm not altogether sure why.
Perhaps it's because, in our sanitised culture, one too often
sees people being led *away* from the sorrows they would be
wiser to face. The impulse to bid farewell to one's dead, to
embrace the corpse that is both the treasury and the travesty

of the life that's gone, is primitive and just. After the battle, however horrendous it has been, we *must* gather up our dead.

It's fitting, too, that Leontes should recognise that something more awaits him in the chapel than 'the dead bodies of my queen and son'. It is *sorrows*; and he is not afraid of them. This (might I suggest?) is Leontes' first moment of real stature in the play. Such a calm assumption of the responsibilities of anguish has hitherto been quite beyond his compass. 'He is now, as never before', writes Wilson Knight, 'kingly' (G. Wilson Knight, *The Crown of Life*, 1965, p.96).

Yet, in the logic of the tale we have so far been told, it can lead nowhere. It is necessarily unavailing, repetitive, unprogressive, statue-like. How can the forward-moving, cumulative energies of the drama find any resolution here?

The stony arrest of grief is something Shakespeare was very much alive to. He had been struck by it in those funerary statues where patience sat on the monument, eternally 'smiling at grief'. And Paulina, before she relents, has given a chilling description of a grief-stricken penitence which has congealed to just such a frozen despair—in a kind of blasting curse which is at least as plausible as her subsequent attempt to soften it:

> Do not repent these things, for they are heavier
> Than all thy woes can stir; therefore betake thee
> To nothing but despair. A thousand knees
> Ten thousand years together, naked, fasting,
> Upon a barren mountain, and still winter
> In storm perpetual, could not move the gods
> To look that way thou wert.
>
> (III.ii. 205)

These benumbed states are the great wintry enemy for Shakespeare. When we next see Hermione she is still locked, where Leontes has left her, in just such a numbness.

And at the end of Act 3, he himself is threatened by the same fate. All our humanity will second any attempt to bring him off. But how is it to be done? Like mad, impetuous Lear, like Othello, like Macbeth, he has imposed his personal melodrama on the world. By what logic can it possibly be taken off again?

· 4 ·

Transitions
Act III Scene 3 to Act IV Scene 2

Like all good composers, Shakespeare has ways of signalling a structural modulation so that, not only is the new key firmly established, but the strangeness of the transition is felt, almost on the nerve-endings. There is a sensation of travel combined with an intuition of arrival. In *Measure for Measure* it goes like this:

> Look, th'unfolding star calls up the shepherd. Put not yourself into amazement how these things should be: all difficulties are but easy when they are known.
>
> (Measure, IV.ii. 194)

In *Hamlet* it is,

> ... So have I heard, and do in part believe it.
> But look, the morn, in russet mantle clad,
> Walks o'er the dew of yon high eastward hill.
> Break we our watch up.
>
> (Hamlet, I.i. 165)

In *The Winter's Tale*, the signposting is even clearer:

> Heavy matters, heavy matters! But look thee here, boy.

> Now bless thyself; thou met'st with things dying, I with
> things new-born. Here's a sight for thee; look thee ...
>   (*Winter's Tale*, III.iii. 108)

The pedal-note, darkly sustained through the storm that
destroys Antigonus and his companions, turns out not to
belong solely to the tragic minor tonality of the First
Movement, but to be also the radiant tonic of the new lyrical
Second Movement.

Structural effects of this kind depend upon being noticed.
The listener is not only to feel the ground moving under his
feet; he is to put it to himself that that is what is happening.
He is to reinterpret the note, and to adjust his expectations
accordingly. Or, in the cases I've cited, the 'composer'
himself is putting it to us—directing attention, pointing
things out: 'Look! Look thee here. Here's a sight for thee!'

As I say, the effect is to be noticed. But if it screams at you,
it undoes itself. For then attention is diverted from the
metamorphic miracles of the daystar, of dawn, or of things
new-born, to the mere ingenuity of the artificer who has
requisitioned the dawn. So that it ceases to be even a real
dawn; it becomes a lighting-effect.

I confess there have been times, reading those famous
lines of the Old Shepherd's, when it has seemed to me that
Shakespeare has shoved a great index-finger in his margin
and scrawled the legend, 'Heere bee Fulcrums!' The
recurrent allusions to the 'old tale' would seem to belong to
the same aesthetic self-consciousness, and to be in danger of
defeating themselves by their very overtness.

It's possible, however, that the feeling of being
manipulated belongs to the reading rather than to the
theatrical experience. And it's certainly true that, in the
mouth of an astonished peasant who has been looking for
sheep and has found a princess—a man torn between elation
and incredulity—the flat antithesis between things dying
and things new-born loses much of its flagrancy and gains
correspondingly in mystery. We know where the 'pretty

barne' came from well enough; but we can also enter, pleasurably, into the bemusement of one who doesn't. The world does contain marvels that make you want to blink and 'bless yourself', and the Old Shepherd initiates us gently into that state of wonder.

Much else in the concluding cadences of the First Movement has been contributing to this effect. I've already mentioned the folkloric music of Antigonus' valediction, with its invocation of benevolent wolves and catering ravens (II.iii. 184). And the 'remote and desert place' to which Leontes consigns his daughter is part of the same fictive landscape. For some reason obscure as it is profound, the very idea of the exposed child left 'to it own protection/And favour of the climate' brings with it a countervailing myth of protection and a hope of deliverance. The association is as old as Oedipus and as universal as the babes in the wood. Leontes himself is not untouched by the spectacle of poignant helplessness, for he uses the diminutive/affectionate 'it' ('it own protection') about the very baby he thinks he detests. And the word 'climate', too, is part of a pervasive vision of the play, about which Wilson Knight has written imaginatively—a vision of man as planted between earth and heaven under that great overarching dome, the 'covering sky', which at once dwarfs and protects his insignificance (see G. Wilson Knight, *The Crown of Life*, 1965, pp. 76–128, *passim*). Under that sky Cleomines and Dion make the prosperous voyage whose speed is 'beyond account'. And from it, 'pow'rs divine' look down to 'Behold our human actions'. The theatre for these actions is being endowed with an epic/mythic vastness.

I wouldn't put it past Shakespeare to have deliberately preserved Greene's geographical solecism—the sea-coasts of Bohemia—with an amused eye upon its fitness for these purposes. It is exactly the kind of unreal geography he needs. The cords of the literal are being progressively slackened, and the 'play' and playfulness of which Leontes was so terrified begins to infect the playwright. As has often

been remarked, Antigonus' dream-vision of Hermione (in
3.3) has a distinct flavour of pastiche, as if Shakespeare were
amusing himself by doing lightly what others had done
lumpishly:

> To me comes a creature,
> Sometimes her head on one side, some another—
> I never saw a vessel of like sorrow,
> So fill'd and so becoming; in pure white robes,
> Like very sanctity, she did approach
> My cabin where I lay; thrice bow'd before me:
> And, gasping to begin some speech, her eyes
> Became two spouts; the fury spent, anon
> Did this break from her ...
>
> (III.iii. 19)

The puppet-like wagging of the head, the gasping and the
'spouts', (not to mention the subsequent 'shrieks' with
which she 'melted into air') contain an unmistakable mild
mockery—but one not without affection for the myth-
matrix it draws upon.

Antigonus goes on to misread the omen in a way that
makes us shake our heads over his fickleness, but the
current of sound feeling continues to run clear:

> I do believe
> Hermione hath suffer'd, and that
> Apollo would, this being indeed the issue
> Of King Polixenes, it should here be laid,
> Either for life or death, upon the earth
> Of its right father. Blossom, speed thee well!
>
> (III.iii. 41)

The incipient blossom-life, indestructible for all its
transient beauty, is here bedded in sustaining soil—
'laid,/Either for life or death, upon the earth'. In matters of
growth man can be no more than a conscientious

husbandman, his limited art dependent on the greater art
that nature makes. Antigonus has performed his part. We
await the flowering and unfolding.

> There lie, and there thy character; there these
> Which may, if fortune please, both breed thee, pretty,
> And still rest thine. The storm begins ...
>
> (III.iii. 47)

The storm does indeed; but it is very short-lived, a brief
convulsion of the expiring wickedness, which is further
distanced by the Clown's rendering of it, just as the tragedy
of Perdita's entry on the world—her 'lullaby too rough'—is
distanced by the Old Shepherd's worldy-wise guess-work
about her origins:

> sure, some scape. Though I am not bookish, yet I can read
> waiting-gentlewoman in the scape. This has been some
> stair-work, some trunk-work, some behind-door-work;
> they were warmer that got this than the poor thing is here.
> I'll take it up for pity.
>
> (II.iii. 70)

We smile for his mistake, but it hardly matters now, since
the pity that the child's plight requires is forthcoming in any
case. The relaxing of unnatural constrictions is proceeding
apace.

Even Antigonus' destruction—in mythopoeic terms, the
punishment of the False Servant who has been instrumental
in the death of the Fair Princess—is given us in comic
transposition:

> I'll go see if the bear be gone from the gentleman, and how
> much he hath eaten. They are never curst but when they
> are hungry. If there be any of him left, I'll bury it.
>
> (III.iii. 122)

Molly Mahood writes, of this scene,

> There is a matter-of-fact acceptance of Nature as it is, in
> the Clown's account of the shipwreck and of Antigonus'
> encounter with the bear. If his vivid descriptions of both
> seem callous, they are in fact only honest; hogsheads have
> more reality for him than have Sicilian courtiers, and he
> sees Antigonus' fate from the bear's point of view. The
> creature must have its dinner, and 'they are never curst
> but when they are hungry.' ... Nature is neither morally
> good nor morally bad; a bear's appetite and a waiting-
> gentlewoman's lapse are accepted as the way of the world.

There is, as Professor Mahood argues, a certain folly in

> regarding everything in Nature as subject to moral
> judgment; and the scenes in Bohemia restore the child's
> or the peasant's freedom from morbid preoccupations
> about good and evil.
> (M. M. Mahood, *Shakespeare's Wordplay*, 1957, p. 156)

This clearing of the air also frees us from *Leontes'* morbid
preoccupations. The stagnant closeness gives way to a scent
of grass and flowers. And to the extent that his notions of
good and evil have proved so very ruinous, we are the more
receptive to other ways of viewing the matter.

All in all, this invitation to take 'heavy matters' more
lightly is timely. The drumming intensity of the drama we
have lived through has created a positive hunger for
deftness, for grace, for some kind of amoral insouciance.
The musical analogy is a happy one here: a completed
movement of tragic power demands, as its complement and
fulfilment, a new departure, a relenting, some reassurance
that humanity has not lost altogether the power of song.

All Shakespeare has to do, to bring off the transition, is to
lure us into forgetting just *how* ruinous Leontes' morbid
preoccupations with good and evil have actually proved.

Stranding us on the sea-coasts of Bohemia, and then sinking
the ship on which we might have escaped back to Sicily, may
be as good a way as any. The communications are cut.
Whatever is now happening to Leontes, *we* are stuck in
Bohemia—a fact which is shortly to be confirmed by the
authoritative figure of Time, the Chorus.

There is another respect in which Shakespeare has been
preparing the soil in which the Perdita-blossom is to be
planted. It comes by way of those very purposeful
reflections on the beginning of human life—the freeing, the
enfranchisement of the 'prisoner to the womb'. And Paulina
takes them one stage further as she allows herself to hang
arrested for a few moments over the cradle, contemplating
the mystery of individuation which is nevertheless a
continuity. As young parents are every day discovering,
there is something miraculous about the reproduction of
oneself—of any self!—in the miniature mirror of a baby.
Even outsiders can feel it: that it can be so tiny yet so human,
so distinct and yet so like!

> And, might we lay th'old proverb to your charge,
> So like you 'tis the worse. Behold, my lords,

(Paulina's demonstrating finger delicately enumerates the
features)

> Although the print be little, the whole matter
> And copy of the father—eye, nose, lip,
> The trick of's frown, his forehead; nay, the valley,
> The pretty dimples of his chin and cheek;

(That prod produces a reflex grin that doting admirers will
never believe to be fortuitous—and Paulina exclaims in
delight and irony,)

> his smiles;
> The very mould and frame of hand, nail, finger.
>   (II.iii. 96)

—which finger, presumably makes its little prehensile clutch upon Paulina's, at this point.

Shakespeare has gone to the trouble, via Paulina's commentary, of endowing his bundle of clouts with real infantine life. And he surrounds it with a familiar adult solicitude and rapture, because the miracle of generation, the 'print' and 'copy' of genetic continuity, is important to his enterprise. Important for what it can elicit in the way of adult generosity and responsibility; but important in and for itself, too, since the 'mind' that the small copy houses always contains the potentiality of a fresh beginning:

> And thou, good goddess Nature, which hast made it
> So like to him that got it, if thou hast
> The ordering of the mind too, 'mongst all colours
> No yellow in't, lest she suspect, as he does,
> Her children not her husband's!

(II.iii. 103)

Paulina's motherly warmth fuses with that of Nature, the good goddess, an everyday deity who attends, in a single act of reproduction, to both conservation and development.

The hopeful, wholesome feeling that suffuse this speech constitute a real answer to the states of frozen stasis—jealousy, obsession, guilt, penitence—that elsewhere threaten the action with destructive arrest. Whatever Perdita, as a grown girl, may turn out to be, childhood in itself contains the potential of life and change.

*

As we embark on the second, more lyrical movement, however, we are reminded that the 'life' will still have to be pursued under the watchful and at times jaundiced eye of the older generation. In Act 4 Scene 2 we re-encounter that generation in the person of the troubled Polixenes.

It is well known that with advancing years the cells of the body don't regenerate with the same efficiency as before.

Perhaps the same is true of the cells of the soul. At the end of Act 3 we have feared it may prove to be the case with Leontes. And Polixenes, at the beginning of Act 4, seems no more to have recovered from the trauma of his visit to Sicily, than Leontes has. The very recollection of it comes over him with a kind of shudder:

> Of that fatal country Sicilia, prithee, speak no more; whose very naming punishes me with the remembrance of that penitent, as thou call'st him, and reconciled king, my brother; whose loss of his most precious queen and children are even now to be afresh lamented.
>
> (IV.ii. 19)

Afresh lamented! The passage of time has done nothing to heal this memory. And with a sideways slip that is very revealing (the move is *via* loss of children), Polixenes goes on to connect a secret wound in his own consciousness with the known wound in his brother's—as if *both* were incurable:

> Say to me, when saw'st thou the Prince Florizel, my son? Kings are no less unhappy, their issue not being gracious, that they are in losing them ...
>
> (IV.ii. 23)

What a violent conjunction this is, when you think about it! There is really no comparison at all between his loss and Leontes'. Yet to this gloomy and (one must conclude) possessive father, the loss is just as total. Indeed, he's so far from any hopefulness on the subject that he can only tackle it by proxy, employing, like Macbeth, 'eyes' under his service to look upon his son's 'removedness'. Polixenes' need of the diplomatically urbane Camillo (who is perfectly well acquainted with Florizel's 'happier affairs' but chooses not to be the first to report them) is acute. His bent for moral melodrama already contains the seeds of violence. Perhaps Camillo can woo him to moderation and convince him that

there are easier ways of taking the freaks of youthful ardour.
Ways like the Countess of Rousillon's for instance:

> If ever we are nature's, these are ours; this thorn
> Doth to our rose of youth rightly belong.
>   (*All's Well*, I.iii. 120)

But then, perhaps he cannot.

It's no more than a sketch, but this short scene (IV.ii)
contains in embryo another familial disaster of suspicion
and mistrust which may escalate into denunciation and
estrangement. Shakespeare has not abolished the
preconditions of tragedy. He wishes them to remain firmly
in view.

All the same, one must concede to Arthur Sewell, that the
disaster is only distantly envisaged:

> the serenity, the acceptance, which mark the vision of the
> Romances is partly, at least, a matter of time-perspective.
> The Romances are plays in which the relationship
> between the generations is seen as a relationship in time,
> and, from one generation to the other, time is seen as the
> dimension in which wounds may be healed and life
> renewed. Time is accepted as the destroyer, because time
> is also the agent of renewal.

The trouble is that such temporal harmonisation may ask us
to suppress what we have known. 'This view of time', Sewell
goes on,

> requires that we should not be too close to the moment of
> destruction, and that we should feel much of the
> sweetness, little of the agony, of the moment of renewal.
> In the Romances, then, it is as though we are looking at
> what happens in time through the wrong end of a time-
> telescope, and Shakespeare presents his characters, as it
> were, in deep focus. It is for this reason that in the
> Romances all the characters are, in a sense, minor

characters, for, being removed from the centre of vision, they lack the depths of psychological perspective and they lack in themselves the immediacy of moral importance, which a closer apperception might have afforded them. They have, in drawing, the sharpness and the simplicity of a miniature.

(A. Sewell, *Character and Society in Shakespeare*, 1951, p. 144)

If serenity is to be purchased at this price, we may wonder, as Sewell explicitly does, whether it is worth it.

Of course, there are many ways in which this account of the Romances is, though ponderable, misleading. The characters do not 'lack the depths of psychological perspective' and the 'immediacy of moral importance' he complains of, though they are arguably 'smaller' than the major characters of the Tragedies. And I shall be arguing that a great deal of the 'agony of the moment of renewal' survives to inform Shakespeare's final scene with power. But I must say that the appearance on stage, in person, of Time the Chorus lends some force to the telescopic analogy. We do seem, rather suddenly, to be looking down 'the wrong end'.

We can only speculate what Time's prologue might have looked like if our text had preserved the earlier appearance that Time himself refers to—the occasion when, so he says,

I mention'd a son o'th'King's, which Florizel
I now name to you ...

(IV.i. 21)

Presumably it opened the play and acted as a framing device for the whole action; but we shall never know.

What *can* be said is that Time is pretty determinedly flippant about his dramatic function:

Of this allow,
If ever you have spent time worse ere now;

If never, yet that Time himself doth say
He wishes earnestly you never may.

(IV.i. 29)

How arch can you get? I don't much like it when authors,
who have spent a great deal of ripe consideration on their
own creations, turn round and invite an audience to treat it
all as 'a waste of time'. It's either a failure of nerve that'd be
better suppressed, or it's cheaply disingenuous and
(possibly) fishing for compliments. However, Shakespeare
has these freaks. He shows a fairly regular disdain for 'this
same mincing poetry', of which he is the one great master.
There are times, apparently, when he'd 'rather hear a brazen
canstick turn'd,/Or a dry wheel grate on the axle-tree'. It's
his own affair, of course, but I don't know that we're obliged
to take him very solemnly when he offers to make it ours.

It's this air of offhand effrontery that makes me reluctant
to read any very deep significance into Time's jingling
pronouncements. It can be done, of course:

I, that please some, try all, both joy and terror
Of good and bad, that makes and unfolds error ...

(IV.i. 1)

Resounding stuff, no doubt. Truth the daughter of Time,
Veritas temporis filia, will give it a philosophical and
iconographical pedigree of some antiquity, if that's what it
needs. It's just that it mistakes the tone. This writing has
none of the stability that marks the purposeful parody of
Gower's speeches in *Pericles*. Shakespeare is fooling about:

         I witness to
The times that brought them in; so shall I do
To th'freshest things now reigning, [Hullo down there,
         Jacobus Rex!]   and make stale
The glistering of this present, [Your humble servant, my
         Lords and Ladies!]   as my tale

Now seems to it. [Aha! thought you had me flat-footed,
    didn't you?]
(IV.i. 11)

If this is the best means Shakespeare has at his disposal to
help him over a hump in his story, he's in pretty bad shape.
But I've mentioned it last, and without enthusiasm, so that it
will be clear how relatively trivial a contribution Time
makes to a continuity that has much deeper organic roots in
the structure of the play. It's a frill, and not much more;
though what it *does* show is an impudent confidence, on the
playwright's part, about the great gaping hole he has left in
the middle of his action. He is so far from being chastened
about it, that he's prepared to spotlight it quite
extravagantly: with a hey presto! and an abracadabra,

I turn my glass, and give my scene such growing
As you had slept between.
(IV.i. 16)

*

I have been stressing continuity, proposing a 'modulation'
rather than a transformation, because I believe it would be a
serious charge against the play to claim that Shakespeare has
given 'the fullest scope to his imagination by taking it
beyond the confines of the world of living, suffering
humanity'. The phrasing is Conrad's, defending himself
against critics who believed he had attempted some such
thing in *The Shadow-Line*. Some of those critics had admired
him for the attempt, and there are, of course, students of
The Winter's Tale who find in its supposed 'trancendence'
the very ground of their admiration. For them, Shakespeare
most shows his genius when he recognises that the
resolution of natural evils must be sought on the
*super*natural plane; and the Romances, seen from this angle,
become a positive advance on the Tragedies, which were
unable to achieve Transcendence. This I can understand,

but I can concur neither with its reading of the play nor with its philosophical premises.

My alternative reading of the play will emerge in the following pages. But it might help if, at this stage, I allowed Conrad to set out for me the alternative philosophical premises.

According to Conrad, the move toward transcendence would not have solved anything in his tale. On the contrary, he says, 'I believe that if I attempted to put the strain of the Supernatural on it it would fail deplorably and exhibit an unlovely gap'. Now the charge that Shakespeare has exhibited 'an unlovely gap' has been recurrent in the criticism of *The Winter's Tale,* and some have seen it as the *result* of putting the strain of the supernatural on the play. Conrad's terms of reference, therefore, his reasons for refusing the supernatural, may help to bring this matter into focus.

> But I could never have attempted such a thing because all my moral and intellectual being is penetrated by an invincible conviction that whatever falls under the dominion of our senses must be in nature and, however exceptional, cannot differ in its essence from all the other effects of the visible and tangible world of which we are a self-conscious part. The world of the living contains enough marvels and mysteries as it is; marvels and mysteries acting upon our emotions and intelligence in ways so inexplicable that it would almost justify the conception of life as an enchanted state. No, I am too firm in consciousness of the marvellous to be ever fascinated by the mere supernatural, which (take it any way you like) is but a manufactured article, the fabrication of minds insensitive to the intimate delicacies of our relation to the dead and to the living.
>
> (J. Conrad, 'Author's Note', *The Shadow-Line,* 1950, pp. v–vi.)

It is possible, then, to entertain the conception of life as an enchanted state without recourse to the supernatural. Not only possible, one may thereby be able to entertain it more richly and subtly. All that's needed is a mind sensitive to the intimate delicacies of our relation to the dead and to the living—there are marvels and mysteries enough there!

No one will dispute that Shakespeare possessed such a mind. Might it perhaps have intimated to him, as to Conrad, that the Marvellous is not consummated by the Supernatural, but betrayed by it into 'fabrication'? Could it be that, even when his art seems to be taking us beyond nature, into some realm of transcendental felicity, even then 'the art itself is nature'—an art as lawful, and as ordinary, as eating?

'Whatever falls under the dominion of our senses must be in nature'—it is one of those tautologies that tell us nothing, and tell us everything. Easy to assent to, impossible to grasp. Human wholeness, however, may well depend upon our believing it.

· 5 ·

The Lambs of Bohemia
Act IV Scenes 3 and 4

If we've been feeling the need of some release into the insouciant eloquence of song, we get it, right enough, with the advent of Autolycus. I've heard it complained that he's no more than a stage gypsy; but, to my ears, the mixture of verve and plangency, the lick and curl of the fiddler's virtuosity, makes authentic music:

> *The white sheet bleaching on the hedge,*
> > *With heigh! the sweet birds, O, how they sing!*
> *Doth set my pugging tooth on edge,*
> > *For a quart of ale is a dish for a king.*

> *The lark, that tirra-lirra chants,*
> > *With heigh! with heigh! the thrush and the jay,*
> *Are summer songs for me and my aunts,*
> > *While we lie tumbling in the hay.*

(IV.iii. 5)

Within thirty lines he has established himself as an improviser as uninhibited as his lark, tuning his voice to the opportunism of the moment, the great song store of the travelling folk providing text and tune for all occasions.

Autolycus's is a world bristling with opportunity:

Every lane's end, every shop, church, session, hanging,
yields a careful man work.

(IV.iv. 675)

For 'careful' read 'carefree': the virtuosity in his thievery, as
much as in his singing, is of the kind that acknowledges no
technical difficulty to exist. It doesn't even bother to
distinguish a church service from a hanging. He no more
acknowledges the obligations of the citizen (to respect his
neighbour's bleaching linen) than he groans under the
obligations of a son. His father conferred his first and last
benefit, one might deduce, when, having 'littered' him, he
named him Autolycus and let him loose on the world. The
son does glance briefly in the direction of
genetic/astrological determinism, 'the imposition
.../Hereditary ours'—being (as he is) 'litter'd under
Mercury'—but it only underlines his humorous freedom to
be 'a snapper-up of unconsidered trifles'.

Our moral solemnities are being systematically defied:

For the life to come, I sleep out the thought of it.

(IV.iii. 29)

Being light-fingered and light-footed ('And merrily hent the
stile-a') seems the only life-style worth cultivating. And
while it's undoubtedly true that there's

not a more cowardly rogue in Bohemia; if you had but
look'd big and spit at him, he'd have run

(IV.iii. 100)

the cowardly flight itself comes to seem part of the same
light-footed adaptability.

As he lovingly milks the Clown of his holiday purse—
'Offer me no money, I pray you; that kills my heart!'—he
shows a positive affection towards his 'sweet sir', his 'good-
fac'd sir', for being so beautiful a gull. With enormous relish

in his Protean skills, he impersonates, in his own rags, a gentleman, robbed by a ragged Autolycus, denouncing the same Autolycus, while he, the real Autolycus, robs the sympathetic soul who is foolish enough to listen to his tale of woe. Since *Richard III*, Shakespeare has never given so spirited a rendering of the joys of dissimulation.

> I'll be with you at your sheep-shearing too. If I make not this cheat bring out another, and the shearers prove sheep, let me be unroll'd, and my name put in the book of virtue!
>
> (IV.iii. 114)

The comedy is entirely disinterested—indulged purely for the fun of it—and yet at the outset its amorality has been quietly identified with quintessential Nature:

> *When daffodils begin to peer,*
> *With heigh! the doxy over the dale,*
> *Why, then comes in the sweet o'the year,*
> *For the red blood reigns in the winter's pale.*
>
> (IV.iii. 1)

The notion of Spring as the irrepressible blush of nature is to be consummated in the person of Perdita, 'peering', like the daffodils, in April's front:

> He tells her something
> That makes her blood look out. Good sooth, she is
> The queen of curds and cream.
>
> (IV.iv. 159)

But Shakespeare states it first in these carefree, rollicking rhythms, so that we shall be in no doubt about its hardiness. The 'sweet o'the year' is in no real danger from 'sneaping winds'—it 'takes' those winds 'with beauty'.

It's the same Shakespearian impulse, I think, which sets the changeling-princess promptly in a direct line of descent

from the Shepherd's earthy old wife. Perdita's shopping-list
(IV.iii. 37ff.) has shown she's no stranger to the kitchen; and
we are next introduced to the Dame in whose school she has
learned the arts of hospitality:

> When my old wife liv'd, upon
> This day she was both pantler, butler, cook;
> Both dame and servant; welcom'd all; serv'd all;
> Would sing her song and dance her turn; now here
> At upper end o'the'table, now i'th'middle
> On his shoulder, and his; her face o'fire
> With labour, and the thing she took to quench it ...
>   (IV.iv. 55)

Here is another of nature's blushes, altogether more fiery.
But it is not snobbishly sequestered from the other. In so far
as Perdita *is* snobbishly sequestered, she is being reproached
for it—'You are retired/As if you were a feasted one'. These
things belong together in this portrait of hospitable
liberality. The bustle, the din, the heat, the egalitarian
goodwill (at either end of the table and on anybody's
shoulder, though they do seem all to be male) are as
naturally fitted to each other as the thirst they create and the
freely flowing liquor that quenches it. It's at the opposite
extreme from a hierarchical or a puritanical order, and yet it
has its own spontaneous orderliness—the old wife 'Would
sing her song and dance her turn,' as custom and impulse
jointly dictated.

Perdita's native style of welcome is differently dictated by
a different nature, as a gift of prepared nosegays, letting
nature speak for her. But it is consonant with the old lady's
welcome in its wish for continuance:

> Reverend sirs,
> For you there's rosemary and rue; these keep
> Seeming and savour all the winter long.

> Grace and remembrance be to you both!
> And welcome to our shearing.
>
> (IV.iv. 73)

Rough country mirth has translated itself into a blush and a
curtsy, but with no loss of substantiality. It is red blood that
reigns in the winter's pale.

*

We have been prepared, in all sorts of ways, to watch
Leontes' abandoned blossom speeding well. There is really
no other expectation in play. Despite Time's coy refusal to
'prophesy', he's given it all away; the girl we are about to see
has 'grown in grace/Equal with wond'ring'. The vital
question for the play's cogency, however, is whether her
kind of 'grace' can gain any purchase on the devastation that
has been left behind in Sicilia. Shakespeare, in writing the
longest continuous scene of his career, is plainly in no hurry
to answer that question. The 'grace' is to receive a very
ample and leisurely contemplation.

Yet for all the leisureliness, something essential to the
contemplation emerges almost at once. If this girl is to have
any effect on the action, it will evidently not be because she
is one of those people who *seek* to have it. She is the very
reverse of a Paulina, who will

> use that tongue I have; if wit flow from't
> As boldness from my bosom, let't not be doubted
> I shall do good.
>
> (II.ii. 52)

In fact, anything done 'for effect' is Perdita's aversion.
Praised as an *ersatz* goddess, she can only regret the folly that
has permitted her to get so 'prank'd up' as to license the
construction. She would chide at the 'extremes' of such talk,
if she weren't sure that chiding becomes her as little as her
'borrowed flaunts' do. She wants to 'borrow' nothing not
her own. In her view, you *should* be able to tell a book by its

cover, which is why she dislikes seeing her princely wooer
'vilely bound up' in 'a swain's wearing'. Florizel may justify
it as much as he likes, with precedents from the jolly
Olympians, but she wants to live in her own unadorned
person, in the real world of real necessities. If she cannot,
she seems almost prepared, now, for renunciation:

> O, but, sir,
> Your resolution cannot hold when 'tis
> Oppos'd, as it must be, by th'pow'r of the King.
> One of these two must be necessities,
> Which then will speak, that you must change this
>   purpose,
> Or I my life.   (IV.iv. 35)

The last phrase—a quiet addendum, as if aside to herself—is
mysterious. You'd expect her to say, '*And* I my life'—the
'change' she must endure being the desolating return to
pastoral singleness, as a consequence of Florizel's changing
his purpose under royal pressure. But her 'Or' shows she has
a different 'change' in mind; that she does not believe she has
yet changed her life at all. 'Or' points to the other
possibility: that Florizel's resolution *can* hold; in which case
she must change her life far more radically. And confronting
that change, she seems to feel an awe bordering on misgiving
which hushes her voice and abridges speech.

Later in the scene, when the two necessities *are*
confronted, I think we are able to see what she was
contemplating here: it was an irredeemable falsity in the
very 'change' Florizel holds out to her as a consummation.
In the wake of Polixenes' furious exit she gathers herself up,
'not much afeard', but absolutely certain what must now
follow. If *this* is the consequence of 'queening it' in vain
imagination, then

> Will't please you, sir, be gone?
> I told you what would come of this. Beseech you,

> Of your own state take care. This dream of mine—
> Being now awake, I'll queen it no inch farther,
> But milk my ewes and weep.
>
> (IV.iv. 438)

This girl, too, knows what becomes a lady like her, and she
will not be shaken loose from it. She does not yet know
quite *what* lady she is, but if she can help it, her life will never
stand in the level of his dreams, or of her own. She had
rather be awake and weep. This Hermione-like simplicity
and stability within the self, this intransigent integrity ('no
inch farther'!) is a crucial ingredient in Perdita's nature, a
bedrock not wholly concealed by the grass and flowers of
her girlish grace.

It is also—though this must be postponed for later
discussion—an integrity which Camillo and Florizel
between them are contriving to subvert; forcing her to
prank herself up yet again, *and* more grievously. Only the
'accident' of her birth, of which they are ignorant, prevents
the subversion being catastrophic.

Outside the crisis situations, however, integrity is most
evident when it's least conscious. It seeks no 'effect', but
neither does it fall into the affectation of seeking to have no
effect. It acts by *being*, and acts all the more profoundly for
that. Up to the moment of Polixenes' 'discovery' we see
Perdita acting upon the people around her in this
unpremeditated way.

One of the effects she has, is to wean her watchers away
from a needless self-consciousness and towards her own
superior naturalness. Florizel is the chief beneficiary of this
contagion of the natural. We see him, at the beginning of the
sheep-shearing feast, a little entangled in his social station,
trying to jest his way out of false consciousness by
parodying himself as a jovial deity in pursuit of mortal
beauty. It doesn't quite answer, since it accidentally
reintroduces the very condescension he is hoping to escape.
In trying not to be Florizel, he has slipped into being an

altogether specious Doricles. And when Perdita brings real
'necessities' to his attention, he dismisses them as 'forc'd
thoughts' which she is to 'strangle' so as not to 'darken ...
the mirth o'th'feast'. Though one never doubts the sincerity
of his affection, he is in a fair way of becoming the prisoner
of the role he has assumed, insisting that everyone shall
'Apprehend/Nothing but jollity'—a truly tedious version of
'mirth'.

Perdita, by being more fluidly responsive to the pressures
of the moment and more in touch with the fluctuations of
her own mood, shows him a better way. For instance, when
the beauty of the flowers she distributes touches her with
the memory of those she *lacks*, and the scale of her wished
bounteousness raises a doubt that nature can match it, a
note of yearning creeps into her voice—why are they all
dim, sweet, pale ... liable to die unmarried? Is transience and
unfulfilment written into nature's contract? But before the
drift of these reflections can 'darken' anything, she recovers
herself with a sigh and a glint of irrepressible humour,
adding (concerning the primroses, 'That die unmarried ere
they can behold/Bright Phoebus in his strength')

> —a malady
> Most incident to maids

(who are deplorably likely to 'die' before properly
married—there's a beautiful blend of innocence and bawdry
in the jest); and she then moves on to the 'bold oxlips,
and/The crown-imperial', her tone becoming itself bold,
like them:

> O, these I lack
> To make you garlands of, and my sweet friend

(that word that so troubled her father, now restored to its
proper freedom)

> To strew him o'er and o'er.

To this plenitude and playfulness of self-giving Florizel rises with a delight that can only take the form of mockery:

> What, like a corse?

And Perdita meet him on that loving ground, with an implicit 'Silly boy!'

> No; like a bank for love to lie and play on;
> Not like a corse; or if—not to be buried,
> But quick, and in mine arms.
>
> (IV.iv. 129)

Love is play. Love is quickness. It is so quick that lovers can even play at death, buried in each other's arms. It envisages no gap, either of scruple or of calculation, between a desire and its fulfilment, for it is an entirely *present* self-giving which lies right outside the categories of jealous possession and self-preservation. Since 'In delay there lies no plenty', it is the incarnation of instant bounty. Above all, in Perdita's speech, it is a kind of coruscating mobility. I can't think of an utterance that more eloquently dispels the notion that had so plagued her father: the notion of chastity and unchastity as mutually exclusive alternatives separated by some carnal act. Florizel is much more 'unchaste' than she, if you like, protesting that his 'desires run not before' his honour—for the protest implies he has lusts to repudiate. Perdita only has feelings to affirm. The fact that they are sexual through and through merely demonstrates their wholeness. She does not share her lover's awkwardness about these things. It seems so natural to her that he should 'desire to breed by [her]' that she can mention it to a stranger without embarrassment—though she does take some pride in the fact that it's her natural unpainted self he so desires.

In the face of this plenitude, I really despair of the misanthropic James Smith when he growls, 'Assurances of that sort are common form with spellbound young women'

(J. Smith *Shakespearian and Other Essays*, 1974, p.156).
Common form? Has he no ears?

There is a unique liquidity about Perdita's emotions and,
as Donne knew, it is precisely when waters

> Kisse one banke, and leaving this
> Never look backe, but the next banke doe kisse,
> Then are they purest.
>
> ('Elegie III: Change')

Perdita's quickened feelings have now achieved that
swiftness and purity that must not be dammed up:

> Come, take your flow'rs.
> Methinks I play as I have seen them do
> In Whitsun pastorals. Sure, this robe of mine
> Does change my disposition.
>
> (IV.iv. 132)

She is *capable* of self-consciousness, certainly—a swift
dishevelled glance in the mirror—but not dwelling on it, not
'looking back', since it is carried by the current of feeling to
the next bank and the next, with the delectable change-in-
stillness of the running stream. I think I would be less
interested in Perdita if she were *incapable* of this
momentaneous reflexive self-questioning. She is right to
distrust the 'robe'. But we can see, as Florizel does, that it
has not changed, so much as released something in her
disposition. Seeing it, helps Florizel to find the true pitch:

> What you do
> Still betters what is done. When you speak, sweet,
> I'd have you do it ever. When you sing,
> I'd have you buy and sell so; so give alms;
> Pray so; and, for the ord'ring your affairs,
> To sing them too.
>
> (IV.iv. 135)

He begs her never to change, and he begs her to go on changing. Wrestling with the paradox of a spontaneity which is so completely *of* the moment that you can envisage no other moment, which moves and is still, he finds the perfect metaphor for the rhythms of its delighted apprehension:

> When you do dance, I wish you
> A wave o'th'sea, that you might ever do
> Nothing but that; move still, still so,
> And own no other function.

> (IV.iv. 140)

There is, of course, no single and distinct 'wave o'th'sea'; there is the sea, and there are dancing waves—'Each changing place with that which goes before', as Shakespeare puts it in Sonnet 60. The sea can be an image of eternal grinding erosion and reclamation—'Increasing store with loss, and loss with store', as in Sonnet 64. But Perdita's wavelike footing takes this classic metaphor for 'devouring Time' and makes it over into an image of eternal renewal. Florizel's love, responding to hers, moves right out of the world of the 'Time' sonnets: it does not afflict itself with transience; it does not 'weep to have that which it fears to lose'. The fleeting essence of Perdita's dancing is no more lost, than a wave is lost in the eternity of change that the sea is. If *she* was a Queen, she might be subject to dynastic violence and accident. But it is her *acts* that are queens, crowning themselves over and over 'in the present deeds'— not subject to the depredations of futurity. Her integrity resides, not in some abstract essence, but in the acts themselves.

I don't think Perdita doubts his sincerity of intent, any more than she is fluttered by his attention. But she is level-headed enough to find the praises 'too *large*'—a word which contains just a hint of indecency (we hear of 'large jests' in *Much Ado* (II.iii. 182), and Cordelia sceptically dismisses her sisters' protestation as 'large speeches'). If Florizel insists on talking like this, she must teasingly address him as 'Doricles' and remind him who he is—or rather who, 'plainly', he isn't:

> But that your youth,
> And the true blood which peeps fairly through't,
> Do plainly give you out an unstain'd shepherd,
> With wisdom I might fear, my Doricles,
> You woo'd me the false way.
>
> (IV.iv. 147)

It's the lightest of rebukes, accepting gracefully, at the same time as it fends them off, the praises. But it removes the last film of artifice from 'Doricles', and he is able to speak at last from the candid centre of the self which doesn't wish merely to admire her dancing, but to dance with her. It is Florizel, true prince and unashamed lover, we hear now:

> I think you have
> As little skill to fear as I have purpose
> To put you to't. But come: our dance, I pray.
> Your hand, my Perdita.
>
> (IV.iv. 151)

Their dance, nicely mingled and counterpointed with that of Mopsa and the Clown, rounds off this section of the scene.

*

Perdita's 'contagion of the natural' is affecting another person present at the sheep-shearing, though his resistance to it is more stubborn. Polixenes, after all, has come with the prime purpose of resisting. Yet, almost immediately, confronted with her clarity of being, his chosen role has him feeling uncomfortably old and stiff:

                    Shepherdess—
A fair one are you—well you fit our ages
With flow'rs of winter.   (IV.iv. 77)

Perdita does not like to be suspected of so much intention in
her gift. She gives what there is to give:

                    Sir, the year growing ancient,
Not yet on summer's death nor on the birth
Of trembling winter, the fairest flow'rs o'th'season
Are our carnations and streak'd gillyvors,
Which some call nature's bastards. Of that kind
Our rustic garden's barren; and I care not
To get slips of them.   (IV.iv. 79)

I don't want to join the horticultural litigation that has
plagued the annotation of these lines. If Shakespeare has
invented a season of the year that never was, that's fine by
me. But the ongoing movement of the drama has uncovered,
revealingly, an instinctive stubbornness in Perdita which
Polixenes' stubbornness promptly seizes upon. Why this
exception? 'Wherefore, gentle maiden,/Do you neglect
them?' Her word 'bastard' should have been answer enough,
but she is obliged, now, to spell it out—and a little
unhappily, I think:

                    For I have heard it said
There is an art which in their piedness shares
With great creating nature.   (IV.iv. 86)

Polixenes has his cue. Wilson Knight's suggestion that he
is 'perhaps setting a trap' (G. Wilson Knight, *The Crown of
Life*, 1965, p. 105) as he defends the very 'piedness' he is here
to prevent, is helpful. Given his mission and purpose, he
could hardly fail to see the bearing of the analogy on the
present case; and he may be hoping to lure Perdita into a
declaration of her own 'seditious' intent. If so, his

argument—that 'nature is made better by no mean/But nature makes that mean'—is too eloquent by half. And as he warms to his task, he seems to be discovering the powerful solicitations of the comprehensive view of nature he had repudiated in Act 1, and which he has come here, again, to render inoperative:

> You see, sweet maid, we marry
> A gentler scion to the wildest stock,
> And make conceive a bark of baser kind
> By bud of nobler race. This is an art
> Which does mend nature—change it rather; but
> The art itself is nature.   (IV.iv. 92)

Whatever Polixenes' real beliefs on this matter, the logic of the generic case is too powerful for Perdita. She can only bow to its abstract cogency: 'So it is'. But she is not a girl to allow mere logic to drive feeling into falsity. She may not be able to defend her aversion, but she is fearless in its authenticity:

> I'll not put
> The dibble in earth to set one slip of them.
>   (IV.iv. 99)

Then, seeing how her intransigence might be construed (like her mother's) as obstinacy, and casting about for the good reason she's sure is there, she lights upon it, with a felicity which destroys all Polixenes' hopes of eliciting sedition from her:

> No more than were I painted I would wish
> This youth should say 'twere well, and only therefore
> Desire to breed by me.   (IV.iv. 101)

If the heir of Bohemia does so desire, the 'sedition' is great creating nature's, not hers. No snare has been set, no piedness cultivated. The 'art' is not hers, but nature's.

Polixenes is silenced it seems; for she turns next, undetained, with her basket of flowers, to Camillo.

The power of Perdita's plea ('Whose action is no stronger than a flower') comes from her consciousness of having no charge to answer. Polixenes may be cultivating an insidious *double entendre*, but Perdita speaks out of the limpidity of her own nature—a purity which is deepened if we notice that it has carried her to denying herself any right whatsoever, as 'a bark of baser kind', except what nature itself bestows.

This is a very different version of 'stronger blood' from the one Polixenes offered in Act 1. Perdita certainly wants her lover. She wants him 'quick and in mine arms'. But no guilt comes with the wish. The impulse itself comes from the heart of an all-embracing Nature. And Nature can be left to generate any necessary prohibitions. There is no need for interference, moral or political. There is enough in Perdita's own nature to prohibit miscegenation—the least suspicion of 'piedness' will end her dream, and she will be content to milk her ewes and weep. So that Polixenes' policing operation is totally redundant. Nature has the matter in hand.

What then is to be the King of Bohemia's relation to that natural creativity? It turns out to be highly, angrily destructive.

The rage Polixenes unleashes against the girl, almost hysterical in its intensity, is powered partly, of course, by pain at his son's indifference to his feelings. It hurts any parent to discover he has been omitted from the love-scenario that the young must always write for themselves (and a Jacobean parent could expect more submission than most in these matters). We have also seen how Polixenes is exactly the parent to invest his son's erotic freedom-of-choice with a perilousness verging on panic.

But when he wants the girl's beauty 'scratch'd with briars', and when he promises, like a more collected Lear, to

> devise a death as cruel for thee
> As thou art tender to't,
>
> (IV.iv. 432)

one catches the accents of a violence being done to the *self*, and not just to the victim. By embodying a 'nature' which dissolves hierarchy in creativity, Perdita strikes a chord of longing in Polixenes. Being human, he is still in touch somewhere with the prodigal amorality of nature. No one ever quite grows out of that golden dream of bounty where all is given, nothing withheld—and *everything* is natural. After all, he has just been playing, with more sincerity than he perhaps knows, its eloquent advocate. Hence, probably, all those notes of involuntary admiration for the girl ('gentle maiden', 'sweet maid', 'the prettiest low-born lass') which continue to sound even in his violences ('excellent witchcraft', 'enchantment', 'beauty', 'tender'). Like all retreats upon a defended uncreative self, his repudiation pains him dumbly with a sense of loss. His ferocity, in fact, expresses the violence of disappointment inflicted upon that part of his nature which desires and fears connection with a larger creative nature.

Well, he says his piece. And those fulminations delivered, he dare not stay for an answer, but must storm out—though we might note in his defence that he does thereby manage the residual tact of leaving Florizel to make his own farewells unaided.

*

In the shocked silence that follows the King's exit, our attention, directed by a kindly Camillo, falls first upon an innocent casualty—Perdita's 'father':

> O sir,
> You have undone a man of fourscore-three
> That thought to fill his grave in quiet, yea,

To die upon the bed my father died,
To lie close by his honest bones.

(IV.iv. 444)

The substantial dignity of the Old Shepherd makes it
natural for him to fall into the cadence and phrasing of a
Macbeth:

If I might die within this hour, I have liv'd
To die when I desire.

(IV.iv. 453)

And then he too stumbles out, leaving Perdita oppressively
conscious of a further unsought falsity—for she *has*, as he
justly charges, 'mingled faith'—she for whom 'mingling' is
so grave a betrayal of essential nature.

Our eyes, like all the eyes on stage, are now upon Florizel.
Whether he accepts the guilt or refuses it, he would seem to
be irremediably in the wrong. Yet he seems not to feel it,
seems almost to be amused by the expectation that he
should:

Why look you so upon me?
I am but sorry, not afeard; delay'd,
But nothing alter'd. What I was, I am.

(IV.iv. 454)

This comes as a relief, but hardly as a solution.

There follows the small comedy in which Camillo (who
has forgotten to remove his disguise) identifies himself, and
Florizel reiterates his determination more trenchantly:

It cannot fail but by
The violation of my faith; and then
Let nature crush the sides o'th'earth together
And mar the seeds within! Lift up thy looks.

From my succession wipe me, father; I
Am heir to my affection.

(IV.iv. 468)

That gallantly assertive 'I', poised conspicuously on the line-
end ... does it represent bravado, or heroism? Shakespeare
is setting the stakes very high, making 'faith' in love
subsume all other faiths, and thrusting aside all the social
codes of 'succession' for the overriding legitimacies of
'affection'. And I've no doubt that, to Jacobean ears, the
revolutionary romanticism of these sentiments would have
been even more striking than it is to ours. Yet I can detect no
admonitory qualification of the sentiments, unless it is
Camillo's pursed lips and mild Tut, tut!—'This is desperate,
sir'—which contains more than a grain of sympathetic
amusement. It is far too weak, anyway, to withstand the lift
and lilt of released, powerful feeling. Florizel is not blind,
either, to the potentially ruinous risk of such courses, for
Shakespeare has him redeploy the images of anarchic
overthrow—the cracking of nature's moulds, the spilling
and tumbling all together of 'nature's germens'—which
were last heard in the Witches' cavern and on Lear's heath.
    The extremity of expression has provoked some critics,
as it provokes Camillo, to head-shaking and to counsels of
moderation: 'Be advis'd', they all murmur. But as Florizel
declines to be, he sounds a note which is to be heard again,
triumphally, at the moment of the play's consummation. Be
advis'd? No. He prefers delusion, if delusion it is, to
anything the 'settled senses' of the world can offer. Be
advis'd?

I am—and by my fancy; if my reason
Will thereto be obedient, I have reason;
If not, my senses, better pleas'd with madness
Do bid it welcome.

(IV.iv. 474)

Good Thomists, like James Smith, turn pale at these accents: this can only be regarded as a 'screaming fit' (Smith, p. 156), and he rather fears Florizel will be damned for it. If so, he will be damned in goodly company, and Shakespeare, anyway, is more at ease than this with 'fancy' and the 'senses', and kindlier disposed to their characteristic madnesses. He has always had a soft spot for those who are capable of

> a wild dedication of [them]selves
> To unpath'd waters, undream'd shores,
>
> (IV.iv. 558)

and he leaves the prudential counselling to the well-characterised practitioner of the *via media*, Camillo—who has, besides, his own axe to grind in this matter and need not be taken too authoritatively.

Unlike his young master, Camillo is not knocked sideways by Perdita's charm. He manages some elderly compliment, it's true—

> I should leave grazing, were I of your flock,
> And only live by gazing—
>
> (IV.iv. 109)

but Perdita takes the pitch of its ornamental pastoralism pretty accurately, when she replies as a practical farm-girl,

> Out, alas!
> You'd be so lean that blasts of January
> Would blow you through and through,

and turns away from him to her 'fair'st friend'. For Camillo she is 'The queen of curds and cream', but he speaks rather as a connoisseur of dairymaids, than as the detector of disguised princesses.

He is similarly staid about the madcap elopement,

indulging some private satire at the expense of this 'more ponderous and settled project' and wondering urbanely whether it 'May suffer alteration'. His value for romantic ardour is strictly provisional:

> Besides, you know
> Prosperity's the very bond of love,
> Whose fresh complexion and whose heart together
> Affliction alters.
>
> (IV.iv. 564)

And when Perdita resists his worldly wisdom—

> One of these is true:
> I think affliction may subdue the cheek,
> But not take in the mind—

he is not greatly abashed:

> Yea, say you so?
> There shall not at your father's house these seven years
> Be born another such.

He will concede that she does seem 'a mistress/To most that teach', but she is nevertheless the sort of 'miracle in nature' that a decent household can expect to occur every seven years or so.

Now, as I've suggested, Camillo can in no sense be treated as a guide to the play's geography. But all the same he is part of a concerted movement in the latter part of Act 4 Scene 4 (Autolycus is another part of it) which is pushing Perdita steadily to the margins of the action, as her freedom of action and liberality of being get progressively eroded. The fountain of youth runs clear, but it isn't, as it used to be in the earlier comedies, the welling source of independent creative power. It is much more contingent and conditional. Contingent upon Camillo—to look no further.

This wise old fox is very much needed by the young
lovers. They have a ship, but no destination. They have
parts to play, but no costumes. They have intentions, but no
plan. Camillo supplies all these commodities, on his own
terms and at his own price. For Perdita, particularly, the
price is high: she must 'retire into some covert', 'muffle' and
'dismantle' herself—in short,

> disliken
> The truth of your own seeming.

(IV.iv. 641)

Dislikening truth is exactly what is most foreign to her
nature; and her submission to these necessities is phrased
curiously, as if it were also,and equally, a submission to the
necessities of Shakespeare's plotting. And she sounds
distinctly unhappy with both:

> I see the play so lies
> That I must bear a part.

In the rest of the 'play' in which she has here agreed to bear a
part, she speaks only three times: once to exclaim in distress
over the plight of her (supposed) 'poor father'; twice, very
briefly, to express respectful veneration for the statue of the
mother she has never known. To the living mother she says
nothing, merely kneels to ask blessing.

It's true of course that a silent character can very well live
on the stage as a bodily presence, and live also in the
reactions and speeches of others—most notably in Leontes'.
But it seems nevertheless unmistakable that Shakespeare,
before the end of the scene where he has profusely created
her, has effectively done with Perdita. What she is and what
she represents has been reabsorbed into the larger rhythms
of the piece. The longish concluding sequence of Act 4
Scene 4 (11.660–830) is given up to a leisurely expatiation
upon Autolycan roguery and Shepherdly simplicity, which
ends by ensuring (as accidentally as possible) that the agents

of Perdita's identification take ship with her, for Sicilia. The playwright who has thus wryly and ruefully submitted his delectable shepherdess to the opportunism of plot, now appears to be satirising that opportunism in the person of the opportunist, Autolycus:

I see this is the time that the unjust man doth thrive ...

Though I am not naturally honest, I am so sometimes by chance ...

If I had a mind to be honest, I see Fortune would not suffer me: she drops booties in my mouth....

(This last *apologia* of the opportunist, by the bye, is delivered over his shoulder as he relieves himself in a wayside hedge.)

There are many reasons—and satisfying ones—why Autolycus is in this play: unimpeded by scruple, he is giving us the amorality of the natural, embodying a freely improvisatory relation to the vicissitudes of life; he is part, again, of a de-romanticised documentary of country life, which must not omit so characteristic a haunter of 'wakes, fairs, and bear-baitings'; he is the ubiquitous spirit of commercial exploitation; and he is the spirit of song—at once parasitic and creative—transforming the miseries of the usurer's wife and the cold-hearted maid into folk epic. But he serves this additional and equivocal purpose of voicing, for his creator, a very conscious unscrupulousness in the conduct of his story.

The fading out of Perdita is, on the face of it, a piece of astonishing wastefulness. Other things, too, are thrown away. We are not even allowed to see her reunion with her father, but get it secondhand, and somewhat sophisticated, through Paulina's steward. One explanation, of course, is that Shakespeare is concerned, not with what the recovery of her parents means to Perdita, but with what her existence means to them—and particularly to her mother. But even that receives sparse treatment. Hermione's blessing, though heartfelt, is brief; and most of what Leontes has to say in praise of Florizel's 'fair princess' is spoken in ignorance of her identity. For him she is simply the reminder and the incarnation of irreparable loss.

After the sheep-shearing feast, there can be no doubt that Perdita's existence matters vastly; but it matters, as it were, in the abstract, not for what other people make of it—not for its 'effect'. Its effect is minimal and minimised. And it is at its maximum when Leontes views her dispassionately—welcome hither 'As is the spring to th'earth'—with no suspicion that he has any claim upon her. It's as if Shakespeare is saying, 'If you want to talk about the renewing restorative power of youth, do so by all means. But it exists, in reality, only in and for itself, or at most, for dispassionate gladness that it does so exist. Nothing can be done with it, and nothing can be made of it.'

It is very much in Shakespeare's mind, at this time, that youth has its own 'brave new world'; but the eye of experience takes in the rapturous delight with a disabling consciousness of not sharing it. As Prospero rather sadly expresses it, observing his daughter's delighted salutation to 'beauteous' mankind,

''Tis new to thee.'

Perdita, of course, is a far bonnier, more individual girl than Miranda. Shepherds make better fathers than magicians. She has her own sensuous and mental identity. But there is a sense in which she still falls, in the latter part of the play, under the paternalistic, not to say jaundiced, Prosperian eye.

Dowden has been much derided for his elderly sentimentalism over the Romances, but one can see what he was talking about when he discerned in them

a certain abandonment of the common joy of the world, a certain remoteness from the usual pleasures and sadnesses of life, and at the same time, all the more, this tender bending over those who are like children still absorbed in their individual joys and sorrows.
(E. Dowden, *Shakspere: His Mind and Art*, 1882, p.415)

In Shakespeare's earlier comedy, the loving voyage of Florizel and Perdita would not have suffered so catastrophic a landfall as theirs threatens to be. They would not have been so subjected to the penalties of hasty planning. When Polixenes arrives fuming, he would have turned out to be, not a baleful and omnipotent patriarch, forbidding the banns, but a misguided and misconstruing Egeus who comes too late to affect anything and is effortlessly overruled. But, as Dowden remarks, those comedies were very different affairs:

> In his earlier plays, Shakspere writes concerning young men and maidens, their loves, their mirth, their griefs, as one who is among them, who has a lively, personal interest in their concerns, who can make merry with them, treat them familiarly, and, if need be, can mock them into good sense.
>
> (Dowden, p.415)

The Shakespeare of Act 5 is no longer 'one who is among them'. His eyes are fixed somewhere else. Hence the relegation of Perdita and the humiliation of Florizel. Hence, too, the faint sense of dissatisfaction which has plagued many readers and estranged some audiences. Why is it that the 'gracious couple', while 'begetting wonder', have so little of the creative elasticity that makes Beatrice and Benedick (say) a transformational power-source in their play? Why is their hope and ardour so easily translated into naïvety in the ways of the world?

Now I know there's no point in wailing that a play is not

something which it never intended to be; but you can still feel that what it *does* intend to be is problematic. It's a question, I suppose, of the value that can be set upon 'experience'. Nobody who has had much of it is likely to believe that it is an unequivocal blessing. Even in that highly 'experienced' play, *The Tempest*, it remains as much a matter of loss, as of gain:

> So glad of this as they I cannot be,
> Who are supris'd withal.
>
> (*Tempest*, III.i. 92)

There speaks a man quite unsurprisable by joy. He has been too long plotting and planning for it. And listening to that despondent cadence, in its leaden fall into unhope, we may well suspect that, as a human good, experience has been somewhat overrated.

Yet, in the closing phases of *The Winter's Tale*, experience seems to be being accorded so much weight, that *in*experience is reduced to the role of a decorative bystander. Shakespeare has in the past, of course, sceptically pondered the possibility that experience is subject to the law of its own self-annulment. But he pondered it in the ebullient person of Rosalind, who notes that the wise men who have 'gained their experience', tend to discover only that their experience has made them sad. Observing this principle at work in the career of the melancholy Jaques, she simply mobilises her powers of mockery to flout at the sadness:

> I had rather have a fool to make me merry than experience to make me sad—and to travel [travail] for it too!
>
> (*AYL*, IV.i. 23)

That was in 1600. Now, in 1610, Shakespeare (and the play with him) seems bent upon travailing for his sadness.

For ours too, in some measure. Why is he so little interested in the young lovers he has so persuasively created? What has happened to the comic resilience of which Rosalind is a heart-warming instance, that it can effect no important change in its world?

Florizel's renunciation of the 'pomp' of Bohemia was not performed out of some paucity of imagination, but out of a sense of fulness. Not all the concealed mysteries of nature were rich enough to tempt him back into social conformity:

> Not ... for all the sun sees or
> The close earth wombs, or the profound seas hides
> In unknown fathoms, will I break my oath
> To this my fair belov'd.
>
> (IV.iv. 480)

And now he is reduced to the glumness of the thwarted schemer. Even Perdita's blush, which had been the blush of spring itself, a language of the blood that 'looks out' boldly and is the very antithesis of shame, is transformed by the false situation into a banal flush of bashful self-effacement:

> Your pardon, sir; for this
> I'll blush you thanks.
>
> (IV.iv. 575)

She has virtually become the boring little shepherdess who can next be patronised as 'My prettiest Perdita'. It's more than a little depressing to see how extensively Florizel has relapsed into the unintentional condescension in which he began:

> My good Camillo,
> She is as forward of her breeding as
> She is i'th'rear o'our birth.
>
> (IV.iv. 571)

'Breeding', in such a context, has become rather shallow and class-ridden, shorn thus of its more vibrant connections with great creating nature.

Isn't there something middle-elderly and defeated about all this, that is unworthy of the writer of those earlier, buoyant comedies? Once again, just as we were getting the hang of the thing (in the sheep-shearing festivities), Shakespeare has shifted the goal-posts.

I know ... this is not a Comedy, nor meant to be. It's a Romance. But that might set us wondering whether Romance isn't another name for a diluted and dispirited Comedy. Or, to put it slightly differently, is Romance perhaps the last mode left to a man in whom the contemplation of Tragedy has extinguished the youthful hope of Comedy?

· 6 ·

The Hypothesis of Hope
Act V

I make no apology for letting the Tragedies loom behind my discussion of *The Winter's Tale*. They do so loom, and that's all there is about it. When you put negative and positive feelings alongside each other it's hard not to find the positive ones flimsy. Maybe it's a sad comment on human life, but there is something in despair that will always seem larger-souled than optimism can ever be. Marvell puts it well, speaking of a love that must remain tragically frustrate:

> Magnanimous Despair alone
> Could show me so divine a thing,
> Where feeble Hope could ne'r have flown
> But vainly flapt its Tinsel wing.
>
> ('The Definition of Love')

The nearer Shakespeare approaches the unveiling of his fable of hope, the more conscious he becomes, it seems, of his Tinsel Wing. It is all, as he insists more than once, 'so like an old tale that the verity of it is in strong suspicion'. Even the staging takes on a highly balletic, choreographic style which could not have been predicted on the basis of the first three Acts. The 'dancers' are forever bowing themselves out with a murmured 'I'll hear you by and by' (IV.iv. 499) or a 'one word' (IV.iv. 586), 'Pray you a word'

101

(IV.iv. 651), to allow other soloists to perform. Asides proliferate. Actors address themselves confidentially to the audience, assume disguises in full view, or pocket up their false beards. The dissimulative aspect of drama is being notably foregrounded. It is required we do awake our faith. But the faith in question seems to be as much a faith in art, as a faith in the regenerative energies of the nature that the art purports to represent.

Now, partly, this is just another aspect of the creative 'play' that was first let loose in Autolycus' songs, and which is so much needed in the world of Leontean obsession; and Shakespeare has, with his usual thoroughness, worked it right down into the grain of his dramaturgy. But I think it may also be a response to a radical truth about Hope—a recognition that it is, in its essence, a hypothetical quality which can only stand aside, autonomous and discrete, from the necessitarian world of Tragedy.

The necessity of Tragedy is the necessity of choice and consequence. Nature presents you with antinomies. You choose; and then, either endure the consequences, or perish under them. There is nothing you can change. It is a case of 'Pour on; I will endure'. Comedy, on the other hand, abhors antinomies. It proposes to bypass consequences. A mistake is no more than a mistake, and only a fanatic will insist on exacting the full penalty for mistakes. After all, the web of our life is variegated with them—

> a mingled yarn, good and ill together. Our virtues would be proud if our faults whipt them not; and our crimes would despair if they were not cherish'd by our virtues.
> (*All's Well*, IV.iii. 67)

On this broad basis of tolerance, comedy proposes a humane absolution.

But can we say that Leontes' mad misprision was 'no more than a mistake'? Hermione, when last seen, was valiantly saying so: 'you, my lord,/Do but mistake.' But it's to be doubted that, even if she had survived the consequences of it, she would still be saying so. The comic absolution that Shakespeare seems about to bestow has come to seem an impertinence. Who dares forgive Leontes?

It's a question which imparts particular interest to Cleomines' opinion that the heavens have already done so, and that Leontes would be wise to follow suit:

> Sir, you have done enough, and have perform'd
> A saint-like sorrow. No fault could you make
> Which you have not redeem'd; indeed, paid down
> More penitence than done trespass. At the last,
> Do as the heavens have done: forget your evil;
> With them forgive yourself.   (V.i. 1)

Shakespeare has sketched, here, the other route his drama might have taken, and the other world where it would have been possible—one where the benevolence of the gods is expressed in the shortness of their memories. It's an appealing notion. Surely humanity can submit to the absolving law of Time, accept gracefully its capacity to blur, soften and mitigate, and so 'shake patiently [its] great affliction off'. Penance may be superseded by a great healing amnesia: Forget! Forgive yourself! ... it's advice that human frailty stands in perpetual need of, and for which Cleomines makes a dignified and humane spokesman. Why can't it be taken? Because it isn't.

It's not just Paulina who, for her own reasons, fights like a tigress against all forgetting. It is Leontes too:

> Whilst I remember
> Her and her virtues, I cannot forget
> My blemishes in them, and so still think of
> The wrong I did myself; which was so much,
> That heirless it hath made my kingdom, and
> Destroy'd the sweet'st companion that e'er man
> Bred his hopes out of ...   (V.i. 6)

As Traversi argues, the phrase 'my blemishes in them', and
the whole barely perceptible pausing and breathing of this
gravely beautiful speech, is recording the inextricable
entanglement of Leontes' guilt with his love (D. Traversi,
Shakespeare: The Last Phase, 1954, pp. 166–7). However
willing he may be to 'forgive himself', he cannot deny *his*
blemishes without losing *her* virtues. For as long as memory
lives on, therefore, as a faithful guardian of emotion, the
'mistake' will remain grievous and indelible.

Which leaves Shakespeare—who remains a comic writer
at least in his wish to alleviate human suffering and promote
human happiness where he can—with only one course: he
must deny the consequences of the mistake. Show them not,
in fact, to have ensued. In honouring the authenticity of
Leontes' guilt, he becomes committed to the hypothesis of
hope.

The course is honourable; but it is also dangerous. The
paying of the tragic penalty had probability, if not necessity,
on its side. But the bounteous cancelling of debts holds no
such inevitability. It can only be hypothetical—'a *chance*
which does redeem all sorows', and one which, as Lear's
plight shows, can never be counted on. 'Redemption' is
always hypothetical in this way—a matter of 'faith'.

Yet the need for some such redemption remains a radical
ingredient in the human soul. We return to the places of our
defeat always with some stirrings of inexcusable hope, 'for
in all of us is the wish to return to the has-been and to repeat
it, that if it were once unblest it may now be blessed'. The
words are Thomas Mann's in *The Holy Sinner*, a fiction of
cyclical restoration that Norman Rabkin very pertinently
adduces to characterise the analogous patterns in *The
Winter's Tale* (N. Rabkin, *Shakespeare and the Problem of
Meaning*, 1981, pp. 121–8).

Mann is right. The wish *is* in all of us. And so very human
an impulse cannot be summarily exiled from literature.
There is a sense in which it is present even in Tragedy,
contributing to its power; for, at the same time as we bow

under them, we are also rebelling against the finalities of Tragedy, importunately demanding the other outcome we know we shall not get. The last Act of *Lear* would lose most of its power if we were not in revolt against the necessity of Cordelia's death. Why should Shakespeare not go out, as a dramatist, to meet this importunacy directly, in an act of supreme fiction? Perhaps the authenticity of the impulse towards restoration can be tested by seeing what it feels like to have it satisfied.

The problem is to find a form for its fictionality. If it is *too* fictive, it cannot satisfy. If it denies its hypothetical status, it simply affronts our sense of reality. The search is for some middle ground. Rabkin, who has given subtle and strenuous thought to this matter, proposes that the middle ground is to be found in a kind of sublime spectacle, one which is interpenetrably both Art and Nature. 'Life as an entertainment for God', he calls it, drawing again on the vocabulary of Mann's *novella*. This reading, he argues,

> explains the otherwise inexplicable insistence in the plays that the life presented as a version of our lives is itself like art, the recurrent suggestion that as people who act we are like actors in a play, the haunting analogies between Prospero's mastery and Shakespeare's, the simultaneous presentation of irremediable evil in a context in which grace triumphs and the potency of evil becomes itself part of an enchanting landscape, a spectacle to amuse us as well as an image of our lives' reality.
>
> (Rabkin, p. 127)

Rabkin's is a satisfying reading, in that it responds warmly to the mitigating benignity of the play's resolution and to its sublime playfulness. More than most critics, he is able actively to enjoy what I've called the 'choreographic' element in the writing. But it is *un*satisfying in the way it discounts the claims of reality upon the action, producing yet another version, I rather feel, of Sewell's 'telescopic effect'. In particular, it implies an experiencing of the events of the last scene in which pain is definitely subjugated to amusement. And the word 'amusement', however Rabkin heightens and refines it, will not, for this reader at least, contain those events. No more than by the last scene of *Lear*, am I 'amused' by the last scene of *The Winter's Tale*.

I believe Shakespeare has plucked his supreme fiction from somewhere much nearer the centre of the pain itself. He has made the experience of loss generate its own prophylactic. And he has done this in two ways: firstly, by dramatising the intolerable and the impracticable in the penitential stasis of Leontes' thoughts; and, more profoundly, by awakening in the audience that exquisite aptitude for hope which lies at the heart of all experiences of loss.

Let me begin with the simpler and more manageable matter. In Act 5 Scene 1 it is given to Dion (the second of the two former envoys to Delphos) to urge the impracticality of the King's present posture. Even if his penitence were not, as Cleomines has claimed, in excess of the trespass, its larger political consequences would still be worrying. While Leontes has been rapturously repenting, the kingdom has been left to fend for itself. Dion very definitely *is* 'one of those/Would have him wed again', as Paulina charges. A disputed succession, in the post-Elizabethan age, was no laughing matter. 'If you would not so,' he retorts,

> You pity not the state, nor the remembrance
> Of his most sovereign name; consider little
> What dangers, by his Highness' fail of issue
> May drop upon his kingdom and devour
> Incertain lookers-on.
>
> (V.i. 24)

This rather masculine version of moral responsibility, in which personal preference and emotional fitness must give way to the common good, is encountered head on by

Paulina's antithetical female version:

> There is none worthy
> Respecting her that's gone.

And there, for Paulina apparently, the matter ends. But she throws in the 'opposeless will' of the oracle, for good measure, and winds up with a version of providence in which political stability is a mere piece of prudential engineering, unworthy to disturb the higher obligations of emotional fidelity:

> Care not for issue;
> The crown will find an heir. Great Alexander
> Left his to th'worthiest; so his successor
> Was like to be the best.
>
> (V.i. 46)

The presence of James on the throne might give this some shadow of respectability, but as political thought it really belongs in the kindergarten.

However, there's an increasingly visible glint in Paulina's eye (and in Shakespeare's too), which suggests that the thoughts on the end of her tongue are not the same thoughts she has up her sleeve:

> Yet, if my lord will marry—if you will, sir,
> No remedy but you will—give me the office
> To choose you a queen: she shall not be so young
> As was your former ...
>
> (V.i. 76)

The battery of heavily underlined 'ifs', followed by a definitive 'shall' which is not at all conditional, would require an exceptionally sluggish audience (of the kind Leontes makes) to pass unnoticed. A nudge is as good as a wink when we are given both, and they are as broad as this.

So that Leontes' subsequent retrenchment on his old
position (out of habit, it would seem) has an air of
obtuseness, in the circumstances:

>   Stars, stars,
> And all eyes else dead coals! Fear thou no wife;
> I'll have no wife, Paulina.

It has all the banal security of the 'home-base'; and if it were
virtuous to be obstinate, we might approve it. But the great
frost has begun to break up, the heralds of spring are at the
door, and we are shortly to see that Leontes' remembrance
has recovered a dynamic quality that is moving forward in
expectation at the same time as it reaches back in regret for
the lost, and indeed fading, reality. The expectation is not so
much a quality arbitrarily introduced, as a repressed organic
energy striving against confinement—an unconquerable
growing need to love the living as well as the dead, and the
living *because of* the dead.

'*Enter Perdita.*' And at the sight of her, something stirs in
Leontes which is not simply regret, something that makes
him reach out involuntarily to *grasp*. His instinctual nature
rouses into renewed activity. If it is true that Florizel's father
will 'grant precious things as trifles', then Leontes knows
what he must beg:

> Would he do so, I'd beg your precious mistress,
> Which he counts but a trifle.

Unconscious of what he's saying to the point of speaking
rather distractedly, he has nevertheless plainly returned to
the restless world of desire and longing. But, by the same
token, he has returned to life. Paulina's rebuke, for the 'too
much youth' in the eye he turns upon Perdita, slides straight
off him. He knows, far below the level of consciousness, the
rightness of the impulse he has just articulated. He wants,
needs to hold, this new Hermione who has been

miraculously delivered from the static world of commemorative remorse and made flesh again. The voice that records his intuition of some buried connection is full of wonder:

> I thought of her
> Even in these looks I made.

What makes this collation of thoughts all the more remarkable is that it is Shakespeare's transformation of the 'unlawful lust' of his source into a kind of regenerative innocence (for Greene's Pandosto vilely assails his unknown daughter with incestuous passion, and subsequently suicides when he finds his mistake). None of this is to Shakespeare's purpose. The love that stirs in Leontes for his daughter is not antithetical to, but continuous with, his love for her mother. Love, on all its possible levels, is an undivided whole: the entire catastrophe was the result of *trying* to divide it into warring factions. And as that great creative continuity puts roots down into Leontes' soul, he finds that he is, remarkably, nothing but a 'friend' to Florizel's 'desires'—a natural ally of young love and young hope.

The reason for this turn-around is that, as he looks into Florizel's plight, it becomes a mirror for half-forgotten experiences of his own. The prince's plea has fallen on unsuspectedly fertile soil. For, as Fitzroy Pyle points out, Leontes distinctly does

> 'remember ... with thought of such Affections', looking at Perdita, and what he remembers is the Hermione he wooed when he 'ow'd no more to Time' than Florizel, whose image stirs in Perdita.
> (F. Pyle, *'The Winter's Tale': A Commentary on the Structure*, 1969, p. 109)

It makes possible a re-evaluation of that (for him) traumatic courtship. And as he relives it, prepossession and paranoia begin to melt away, revealing a simpler outline. The process comes to completion before Hermione's 'statue'. There is a small resistant convulsion from the idealising imagination, which has made the real woman over into a sentimental myth—'as tender/As infancy and grace'. But he accepts the 'wrinkles', steadies himself in his present, and suddenly those 'crabbed months' of soured memory dissolve, like the miasma of misconstruction they always were, and he remembers what he has hitherto suppressed—the *warmth* that lay in her very 'majesty':

> O, thus she stood,
> Even with such life of majesty—*warm* life,
> As now it coldly stands—when first I woo'd her!

She was not then, and she isn't even now, made of stone. His emotion before the 'statue' proves him wrong on both counts, and he weeps, helplessly, like a child, but, like a child, not hopelessly.

The unlocking of these frozen springs of feeling has been proceeding throughout the scene. It is grounded upon Leontes' courageous willingness, not merely to commemorate but to re-experience his loss, even if he risks his own sanity in the process. It is cruel to be reminded that the dead Mamillius and the living Florizel are near twins—

> there was not full a month
> Between their births.

The thought threatens to

> bring me to consider that which may
> Unfurnish me of reason.   (V.i. 122)

But it may be necessary. And Leontes' capacity to *have* these feelings, in all their anguish, is growing by the moment as he exercises it. He almost seems to be embracing the pain of returning life:

> Most dearly welcome!
> And your fair princess—goddess! O, alas!
> I lost a couple that 'twixt heaven and earth
> Might thus have stood begetting wonder as
> You, gracious couple, do.
>   (V.i. 130)

'Though bearing misery', he still 'desires [his] life' to look upon these things. He has as yet received nothing for his personal consolation, and yet the rhythms and intonation of these lines speak far more of joy than of misery. It is an intuitive joy at the ending of the great winter, beside which the personal pangs fade into insignificance.

*

I think it is because Shakespeare *knows* he has done all that is necessary to portray the invincible upward surge of hope in Leontes' injured yet unmaimed soul, that he dispenses with the actual reunion of father and daughter. Why stage it? We have been given the essential dynamic. Its literal enactment is unnecessary. It can be sketched in, in those accents of amused urbanity that opened the play—the voices of civilised, faintly effete men, rather surprised at the exorbitance of their own sentiments, though quite certain of their solidity. We in the audience, anyway, are presumed to have foreseen it all too thoroughly to need it spelling out. Its joyfulness is most eloquent if left tactfully implicit.

And the anonymous Gentlemen make possible a further tact. For joyfulness of this order can only be known to those who experience it. The rest of us are no more than tolerated bystanders, likely at any moment to be 'commanded out of the chamber'. The best way of honouring the emotion of the participants is to recognise that we can't begin to know what it is:

A notable passion of wonder appeared in them; but the wisest beholder that knew no more but seeing could not say if th'importance were joy or sorrow—but in the extremity of the one it must needs be.

(V.ii. 15)

One reason we can't know, of course, is that this is a passion which, like most large passions, disposes permanently of the dichotomy between joy and sorrow. We have entered a region where the distinction is unreal. It is both. It is neither. It is itself.

In these ways, before he knows any reason for it, Leontes had begun to feel the breathless possibility of resuming the interrupted continuities of living and loving. And once the dam of unhope is breached, there is no limit to the miracles he can countenance. He is like a child who, after one incredible treat, goes limp with pleasure at the thought of what may follow:

> What you can make her do
> I am content to look on; what to speak
> I am content to hear; for 'tis as easy
> To make her speak as move.

(V.iii. 91)

All the adult categories of probability have been abandoned. What can he know any more, about the possible and the impossible, when what was lost has begun to be found?

But there is something more here than the poignancy of undeserved blessedness. As I said, the exquisite aptitude for hope is born out of the heart of the experience of loss itself, and it has a strength, consequently, which is a great deal more than mere poignancy.

Anybody who has suffered a bereavement can tell you what a tumult of distress and rapture can be stirred up by an unexpected snapshot, the sight of a face in the crowd, or a retreating figure which looks as if it might just have been the dead beloved. It can take years for this propensity to die with the dead. It is a radical ingredient in the human soul. And you will follow that retreating figure, knowing perfectly well that you're cultivating a delusion, yet preferring that delusion to anything the world can offer you in the way of solid reality. It is enough to feel again what you have been prevented for so long, by brute fact, from feeling—what you have feared you may never feel again. That it is almost pure pain is negligible, beside the heart-stopping sense of recovery and recapture. It's a pain for which you are hungry.

Leontes feels that, and he makes us feel it. His affliction 'has a taste as sweet/As any cordial comfort'. This is common ground. We gaze into the snapshot. We play and replay the tape-recording. Well-wishers try to stop us lacerating ourselves. We shove them aside:

> Let be, let be.
> Would I were dead, but that methinks already—
> What was he that did make it? See, my lord,
> Would you not deem it breath'd?

It cannot be but that the statue 'has motion in't'. Maybe we only 'think' it has. Maybe we've put it there ourselves. But we no longer care:

> O sweet Paulina,
> Make me to think so twenty years together!
> No settled senses of the world can match
> The pleasure of that madness.
>
> (V.iii. 70)

Certainly this love is 'madness'. But how can Leontes, any more than the Florizel he re-echoes, prefer the banality of 'settled senses'? Poised between hope and despair as he is, it is impossible to say whether he is re-experiencing the loss, or feeling the first taste of restoration on his tongue. Fearing both, all he can desire is the infinite prolongation of the moment.

So that the tiny impulsion that transforms the Artifice of the statue into the Nature of a living, breathing Hermione, comes neither from Leontes nor from Shakespeare. It is the inevitable, the only just response of the spectators, to an intolerable rapture of impossible possibility—if it could only be ... it cannot be ... it must be. In this way, the humane generosity of the audience is enlisted, to wish for Leontes what he dare not wish for himself. And as the tide of fellow-feeling flows into the empty places of his life, the miracle is accomplished without noise or ostentation. Failing to wish it otherwise, we are bound to wish it thus.

It remains a hypothesis, of course—but an extremely tender one. Tender over human distress; tender in its application of retributive doctrines to those who have already sufficiently suffered; tender over anything that still retains the potentiality for emotional warmth and fulfilment. To deny that potentiality is to deny something in ourselves. The supreme fiction has triumphed, not by defying but by expressing the realities of the human psyche that demand such a fiction. Those realities are as much ours as Leontes'.

· 7 ·

An Art Lawful as Eating
Act V Scene 3

I don't want to encumber the play with much more commentary. I hope that, by now, readers will be impatient to be done with criticism and to become readers of Shakespeare again. But there are ways in which the final scene does draw the drama together—as well as meeting many of the objections I have been raising along the way. So it seems proper to add a few final remarks.

The royal party gathers, 'with all greediness of affection', at Paulina's 'removed house'—which, as a heavily significant Second Gentleman tells us, 'she hath privately twice or thrice a day, ever since the death of Hermione, visited'. By now the benign drift of the story has become pretty overt. We may not know exactly what to make of the fabled statue that 'would beguile nature of her custom', but we are pretty sure that the 'rare Italian master, Julio Romano' hasn't got a lot to do with it. And as our stirring hopes converge with the latent hope which the return of Perdita has awakened in Leontes, so Paulina's presiding role converges more and more with the playwright's. There have been problems with her as a spiritual adviser, and even more with her role as political duenna, but once she becomes a straightforward 'presenter' who seats her audience, draws curtains and calls for music, they largely evaporate. Her proprietorial fussing over the presentation, her pretended worries about the

115

'newly fix'd' colours, and her fears that the 'oily painting' may stain her guests, constitute together a kind of gentle parody of Shakespeare's own stage-manager's solicitude over the reception of his creation. Like Jane Austen in similar situations, Shakespeare finds it easiest to express his own participatory warmth by very nearly appearing in person at the concluding festivities. He wants it to be understood that if he mocks us with art, it is with no intention to deceive, but rather to put us on the same footing with him. We are to enjoy, as coadjutors, the pleasures of a liberated creativity.

Yet the creativity is not liberated from *all* restraint. It's both significant and moving that, even while Hermione hangs about Leontes' neck, she can find no word to speak to him, nor he to her. What, in such a case, could the words be? When she explains the ending of her long seclusion, she does not attribute it to the desire to be reunited with her husband. It would not be true. They could have been reunited any time this last sixteen years. She has preserved herself, in truth, as she says, to see the issue of the oracle concerning Perdita, and only to Perdita does she speak.

There is an impressive austerity in this. Shakespeare, rigorous to the point of chilliness, will not minimise the scale of the repairs this relationship must now undergo. There are barriers between husband and wife that can only slowly be dismantled. The discovery that he is not, in fact, the murderer of their daughter, brings down the first of them, makes it possible for Hermione, silently, to open her white hand once again. But it is only the first of them.

Nevertheless, the interpretation of Shakespearian silences calls for delicacy. They cannot simply be construed as sullennesses. That was the youthful misunderstanding Telemachus fell into when he saw that his mother could find nothing to say to the returned Odysseus, but sat on the opposite side of the hearth, 'overwhelmed with wonder'. To the young man, not having observed her other language of glance and gesture, such behaviour showed her to be a 'strange, hard-hearted mother', one whose heart 'was always harder than flint'. He is very wrong; and Penelope has to put him right at least about the state of her heart:

> My child, the shock has numbed it.... I cannot find
> a word to say to him; I cannot ask him anything at all;
> I cannot even look him in the face. But if it really is
> Odysseus home again, we two shall surely recognise each
> other, and in an even better way; for there are tokens
> between us which only we two know and no one else has
> heard of.
>
> (Homer, *Odyssey*, Book xxiii, trans. E. V. Rieul, edn, 1946,
> pp. 354–5)

Numbness doesn't depart in an instant. The return of sensation can be slow and painful. One would be less certain of its reality, indeed, if it came too quickly. But hidden within the pain is 'an even better way'—a secret recognition, 'tokens between us', which may in time become joyful.

For Shakespeare, too, the better way has to be something surer and more trustworthy than words. And he finds it in the language of touch and embrace. Just as the reality of Cordelia reaches Lear, bound upon his wheel of fire, through the tips of his fingers, as he reaches up incredulously to touch her cheek—

'Be your tears wet? Yes, faith'—

just so the reality of Hermione reaches Leontes as he overcomes the fear that has almost made him shy away from contact altogether, and takes, tremblingly, the hand she holds out to him. Then comes the quick intake of breath, the rush of certainty overbearing his incredulity, and that ecstatic cry which is both absurd and heart-breaking in its discovery of the obvious:

'O, she's warm!'

Poor Leontes! To be obliged to fetch such a circuit of anguish before he can know this simple truth, which always was the truth about Hermione. But by the same token, how far-from-simple a truth it must be if it can dissolve at a single touch all those years of anguish. It's one of Shakespeare's greatest distinctions as a playwright, to know how profoundly our sense of value is rooted in the language of touch. Even a Coriolanus can feel its overriding authenticity, its power to dissolve and transmute, as Virgilia reaches up to her estranged husband's lips:

> O, a kiss!
> Long as my exile, sweet as my revenge!

And suddenly all the structures of military domination crumble into insignificance.

You might almost say that this is the single most important discovery of *The Winter's Tale*—the discovery of warmth. The word echoes throughout the last scene. And perhaps its most healing aspect is its simplicity as sensation. In that absolving simplicity, its adversary, numbness can be finally bequeathed to death where it belongs. Stone becomes flesh. Dear life redeems it. Breath parts the lips that seemed eternally stilled, for 'The very life seems warm upon her lip'. If Leontes, after that embrace, has very little to say, it is because he has only one thing to say, only two words left in his vocabulary: 'warm life'. And the wonder of that subsumes everything else.

He does, however, as he dazedly comes to, find a few other words—distracted, disjointed words, as he stares about him at all these dear people for whom he must do something ... but what is it to be? In this whirl of emotion (beneath which the last sixteen years appear to have sunk without trace), it can only be one thing: marriage. Marriage is the great panacea. How does he know? Becase it has been so, for him, for at least the last sixty seconds. Paulina, poor old turtle, cannot be left grieving and unmated! There must

be someone ... ah, Camillo! (I *partly* know his mind) Would
that be right? ... Yes? ... YES! Here, Camillo, take her by the
hand. There is no way this can be staged without its touching
clumsiness being highlighted. But who is going to object
now ... if it makes him happy ...?

And Polixenes? How terrible? Polixenes is avoiding
Hermione's eye, and she is declining (perhaps out of tact) to
meet his. This too must be put right. At once!

> What! look upon my brother. Both your pardons
> That e'er I put between your holy looks
> My ill-suspicion.

> (V.iii. 147)

And who's this? Of course! Florizel. And he's a stranger to
Hermione. Perhaps she hasn't yet been told of this crowning
felicity? And it all comes tumbling ungrammatically out:

> This your son-in-law,
> And son unto the king, whom heavens directing,
> Is troth-plight to your daughter.

It's all too much for Leontes. He is walking on fire, bathed in
bliss. There is so much still to know. He needs leisure, and
all he feels is the overwhelming haste of trying to do, to take
in, to lay hold of, everything at once:

> Good Paulina,
> Lead us from hence where we may leisurely
> Each one demand and answer to his part
> Perform'd in this wide gap of time since first
> We were dissever'd. Hastily lead away.

So ends the play. It's one of the most distracted, fumbled,
urgent inconclusions Shakespeare ever permitted himself.
Leontes was never more absurd. But the absurdity is called
Happiness—the extremity of both joy and sorrow, self-

accusation mingled with a growing confidence that the disseverance is past and the wide gap of time is beginning, just beginning, to close.

I think Shakespeare is able to give such ample play to the comical and the farcical in his denouement, because he has laid his foundations so securely. For there is one great structural rhyme that spans the entire action like an arch. The stony figure who descends from the pedestal and presents her hand is a sublime travesty of the supposedly unresponsive Hermione who, before the play began, was so slow to open her white hand and clap herself his love. But the traumatic wound of Leontes' misconstruction is being healed, as the roles are reversed, and he discovers in his *own* feeling a reluctance of awe before the magnitude of the commitment, which had been perhaps a part of *her* reluctance when he wooed her. To take the hand of the living, sentient Hermione is a momentous step, because, this time, he must not let it fall in mistrust and recreate the conditions of their long disseverance. Paulina, actually, has to do a bit of pushing from behind:

> Do not shun her
> ... Nay, present your hand.
> When she was young you woo'd her; now in age
> Is she become the suitor?

(I think Folio's question-mark has the force of an exclamation, here.) But she has grasped and articulated the ceremonial significance of the repetition, the closing of the circle. Completion is at hand. 'In all of us is the wish to return ... to repeat ... that if it were once unblest it may now be blessed.'

The hand he takes into his touch is 'warm'. When he was merely watching it, in Act 1, it had been 'too hot'—because he had stopped holding it. There is a prurience in the merely visual which can easily mislead. When watching gets separated from feeling, it turns rancid. The imagination

extrapolates and magnifies, overheats for lack of the true
material of its apprehension. Before long it has separated
sexuality from the main body of life and turned it into a
thing of terror, endowing it with portentous isolation. It is
thus magnified to unmanageable size and intensity *and*, at
the same time, belittled by being severed from the living
tissue of bodily existence. One must take the hand again,
feel its warmth, which is the warmth, not of an 'it', but of a
'she'—of the whole person. And then, magically, there is no
magic any more, just a sublime ordinariness:

> O, she's warm!
> If this be magic, let it be an art
> Lawful as eating.

There are anti-climaxes in literature richer than any
climax can hope to be. This is one of them. It's like Donne
discovering, with wry delight, that his love is not 'so pure' a
he had thought it was,

> Because it doth endure
> Vicissitude and season, like the grass.

O, what a catastrophe! There is something better, in the end,
than love's infiniteness; it is 'Loves Growth' as an organic
part of the elemented world of grass, water and blossoms
which flourishes, down here, under the working vigour of a
terrestrial sun. Who needs purity? It is an art lawful as eating
that Leontes finds has been restored to him, in all its
astonishing naturalness. The artificial 'disseverance' of
things that belong together is at an end, and the reintegration
of that manifold thing called 'love' has begun.

*

I have allowed full weight to the misgivings excited by the
peculiar route the play follows to this resolution of its

difficulties, because I believe puzzlement along the way is part of the audience's experience. But the magnitude and rightness of the truth that is recovered may well swamp all misgiving. It may not matter in the least that Florizel and Perdita are mere spectators of the recovery. The next generation will follow its own course among its own difficulties. It doesn't make them negligible to allow that they are different. In a way, it simply enhances the play's unity, that it holds its final focus steadily on the Leontean problem initially propounded. Possibly nothing else would have satisfied—and certainly not some delegation of the problem to the next generation, for solution.

But perhaps Shakespeare's greatest achievement, in this scene, is to find the perfect mode for the fictionality of his ending. It is Art through and through, but an art that knows its own limits. It can never create a life that actually breathes. For that, it remains permanently dependent upon nature:

> Still, methinks,
> There is an air comes from her. What fine chisel
> Could ever yet cut breath?

But by concentrating on the moment of transition—stone into flesh—the moment of 'breath'—Shakespeare has come as close as anyone can to having it both ways. It cannot happen, but if it could happen, it would feel like this. Since it does, so vividly, feel like this, perhaps it can happen.

At this point of exquisite equipoise, he summons his last resource, the metamorphic miracle-worker, music— coactive with what's unreal, it's true, but not in the nightmare fashion of jealous delusion. Only music can make real the unreal in a way that reintegrates it with the creative continuum, awakening, uniting, redeeming. It will be slow, halting, painful—this musical summoning of the numbed soul out of the great frost of matter—but it is the miracle of miracles. Paulina's grave pavane of conjuration is the play's true climax (and I give it with the Folio's pointing,

where the tempo and pausing is most clearly indicated, a
Lento Maestoso of quite wonderful spaciousness):

> Music; awake her: strike: [*Music*]
> 'Tis time: descend: be stone no more: approach:
> Strike all that look upon with marvel: come:
> I'll fill your grave up: stirre: nay, come away:
> Bequeath to death your numbness: for from him
> Dear life redeems you.

'Dear life'. Costly to an extent that has seemed exorbitant
in the course of this play, but to be valued according to the
cost, now the purchase is complete. But life is also 'dear'
because it is intimate, familiar, trusted—a matter of hands,
lips, eyes and breath—an ordinary miracle of great creating
nature's.

It is that life, doubly dear, and only that life, that can
'redeem'.

Bibliography

C. L. Barber, '"Thou that beget'st him that did thee beget":
Transformation in *Pericles* and *The Winter's Tale*',
Shakespeare Survey 22 (1969), pp. 59–67.

A. Barton, 'Leontes and the Spider: Language and Speaker
in Shakespeare's Last Plays', in P. Edwards, I.-S.
Ewbank and G. K. Hunter (eds), *Shakespeare's Styles*,
Cambridge 1980.

D. Bartholomeusz, *The Winter's Tale' in Performance*,
Cambridge 1982.

S. L. Bethell, *'The Winter's Tale': A Study*, London 1947.

S. Booth, 'Speculations on Doubling', in *'King Lear'*,
'Macbeth', Indefinition and Tragedy, New Haven 1983,
pp. 129–55.

G. Bradshaw, *Shakespeare's Scepticism*, Brighton 1987, pp.
80–94.

G. Bullough, *Narrative and Dramatic Sources of Shakespeare*,
London 1973, vol. 8.

S. T. Coleridge, *Shakespearean Criticism*, ed. T. M. Raysor,
London 1960.

E. Dowden, *Shakspere: his Mind and Art*, London 1882.

P. Edwards, 'Shakespeare's Romances: 1900–1957', in
Shakespeare Survey 11 (1958), pp. 1–18.

H. C. Goddard, *The Meaning of Shakespeare*, Chicago 1951,
II, pp. 262–76.

125

H. Granville-Barker, *Prefaces to Shakespeare*, London 1974, vol. 6, pp. 19–25.

W. Hazlitt, *Characters of Shakespeare's Plays*, London 1817.

S. Johnson, *Johnson on Shakespeare*, Oxford 1908.

G. Wilson Knight, *The Crown of Life*, London 1948, ch. 3.

L. C. Knights, '"Integration" in *The Winter's Tale*', *Sewanee Review* 84 (1976), pp. 595–613.

J. Lawlor, '*Pandosto* and the Nature of Dramatic Romance', *PQ* 41 (1962), pp. 96–113.

F. R. Leavis, 'The Criticism of Shakespeare's Late Plays: A Caveat', in *The Common Pursuit*, London 1952.

M. M. Mahood, *Shakespeare's Wordplay*, London 1957, ch. 7.

J. Masefield, *William Shakespeare*, London 1912.

K. Muir (ed.), '*The Winter's Tale*': a Casebook, London 1968.

J. Middleton Murry, *Shakespeare*, London 1936, ch. 18.

D. J. Palmer (ed.), *Shakespeare's Later Comedies*, Harmondsworth 1971.

F. Pyle, '*The Winter's Tale*': A Commentary on the Structure, London 1969.

N. Rabkin, *Shakespeare and the Problem of Meaning*, Chicago 1981, ch. 4.

A. Sewell, *Character and Society in Shakespeare*, Oxford 1951, ch. 7.

J. Smith, *Shakespearian and Other Essays*, Cambridge 1974, ch. 6.

F. C. Tinkler, '*The Winter's Tale*', *Scrutiny* 5 (1937), pp. 344–64.

D. Traversi, *Shakespeare: The Last Phase*, London 1954.

G. Wickham, 'Shakespeare's Investiture Play', *TLS*, 18 December 1969.

Index

#29/sc